PUPIL
TEXTBOOK
4A

Noogol

Googol

Koogol

Ooogol

Zoogol

Toogol

Consultant and author
Dr Fong Ho Kheong

Authors
Chelvi Ramakrishnan and Gan Kee Soon

UK consultants
Carole Skinner, Simon d'Angelo and Elizabeth Gibbs

Published by Marshall Cavendish Education
Times Centre, 1 New Industrial Road, Singapore 536196
Customer Service Hotline: (65) 6213 9444
Email: tmesales@mceducation.com
Website: www.mceducation.com

Distributed by
Oxford University Press
Great Clarendon Street, Oxford,
OX2 6DP, United Kingdom
www.oxfordprimary.co.uk
www.oxfordowl.co.uk

First published 2015

ISBN 978-981-01-8886-3

Printed in China

Acknowledgements
Written by Dr Fong Ho Kheong, Chelvi Ramakrishnan and Gan Kee Soon

UK consultants: Carole Skinner, Simon d'Angelo and Elizabeth Gibbs

Cover artwork by Daron Parton

The authors and publisher would like to thank all schools and individuals
who helped to trial and review Inspire Maths resources.

Introduction

Inspire Maths is a comprehensive, activity-based programme designed to provide pupils with a firm foundation in maths and to develop the creative and critical thinking skills to become fluent problem solvers.

Inspire Maths makes learning maths fun and rewarding through the use of engaging illustrations and games that help to reinforce and consolidate learning.

For the teacher:

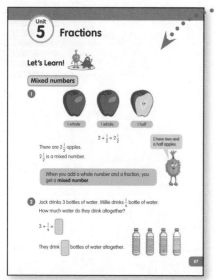

Use the engaging and highly scaffolded **Let's Learn!** to introduce concepts. Integrated questions allow for immediate assessment and consolidation of concepts learnt.

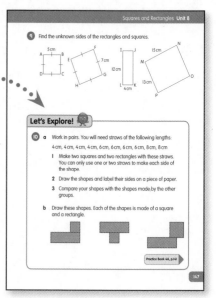

Carry out investigative activities in **Let's Explore!** These allow pupils to apply concepts learnt.

Challenge pupils to solve non-routine questions by applying relevant heuristics and thinking skills in **Put On Your Thinking Caps!**

For the parent/guardian:

Build home-school links and make maths come alive by using the tips in Home Maths to help children apply mathematical concepts to daily life.

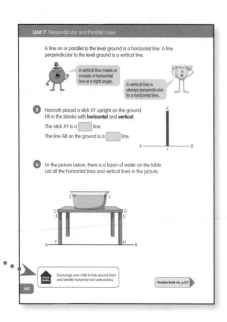

For the pupil:

Enjoy **Inspire Maths** with your friends. Explore your learning through activities and games.

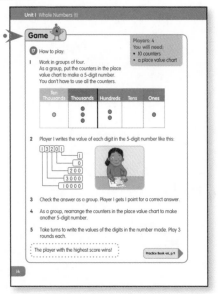

Share what you have learnt, create your own questions and become aware of your own mathematical thinking in your **Maths Journal**.

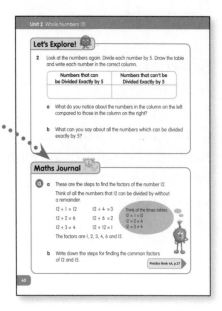

Contents

1 Whole Numbers (I)

Let's Learn!

Numbers to 100 000

1 1000, 2000, 3000, 4000, 5000, 6000, 7000, 8000, 9000, $\boxed{10000}$

Read the numbers.
What number comes next?

10 000
ten thousand

	Ten Thousands	Thousands	Hundreds	Tens	Ones
9000	OOOOO OOOO	●●●●●● ●●●●	OOOOOO OOOOOO OOOOOO		

	Ten Thousands	Thousands	Hundreds	Tens	Ones
10 000	O	OOOOOO OOOO	OOOOOOOOOOO OOOOOOO		

10 thousands = 1 ten thousand

2 Read and show the numbers I5 000 and 73 486 in place value charts.

a

15 000
fifteen thousand

Ten Thousands	Thousands	Hundreds	Tens	Ones
I	5	0	0	0

b

73 486
seventy three thousand, four hundred and eighty-six

Ten Thousands	Thousands	Hundreds	Tens	Ones
7	3	4	8	6

3 What are the missing headings?

12 059
twelve thousand and fifty-nine

I	2	0	5	9

4 Write in words.

Ten Thousands	Thousands	Hundreds	Tens	Ones
5	6	8	I	7

5 Write in numbers.

ten thousand, two hundred and seventy-three

Ten Thousands	Thousands	Hundreds	Tens	Ones
5 ✓	6 ✓	8 ✓	I ✓	7 ✓

6 Read the number pattern. What number comes next?

10 000, 20 000, 30 000, 40 000, 50 000,

60 000, 70 000, 80 000, 90 000, 1 00 000 ✓

What comes immediately after 99 999?

100 000
one hundred thousand

10 ten thousands = I hundred thousand

7 Write in words.

a 47 048   b 90 015   c 86 300   d 70 005

Home Maths

Remind your child that to write in numbers we use the digits 0 to 9 to make the number.
For example, in words "sixty two thousand", in numbers "62 000".

Practice Book 4A, p.7

Activity

8 You will need some play money:
Five £10 000 notes Ten £1000 notes Five £100 notes Ten £10 notes
Make these amounts and ask your friend to check your answers.

a £24 180   **b** £59 470   **c** £37 590

9 Look at the number 31 798.

Ten Thousands	Thousands	Hundreds	Tens	Ones
⚪⚪⚪	⚫	⚫⚫ ⚫⚫ ⚫⚫ ⚫	⚫⚫⚫ ⚫⚫ ⚫⚫ ⚫⚫	⚫⚫ ⚫⚫ ⚫⚫ ⚫⚫
3	1	7	9	8

> thirty one thousand, seven hundred and ninety-eight

In 31 798:
the digit 3 is in the ten thousands place.
the digit 3 stands for 3 ten thousands or 30 000.
the value of the digit 3 is 30 000.

the digit 1 is in the thousands place.
the digit 1 stands for 1 thousand or 1000.
the value of the digit 1 is 1000.

the digit 7 is in the hundreds place.
the digit 7 stands for 7 hundreds or 700.
the value of the digit 7 is 700.

the digit 9 is in the tens place.
the digit 9 stands for 9 tens or 90.
the value of the digit 9 is 90.

the digit 8 is in the ones place.
the digit 8 stands for 8 ones or 8.
the value of the digit 8 is 8.

10 Answer these questions.

    a   In 42 653, the digit ⬜ is in the ten thousands place.

    b   In 63 971, the digit 9 is in the ⬜ place.

    c   In 20 974, the digit in the thousands place is ⬜.

    d   In 56 301, the value of the digit 3 is ⬜.

    e   In 70 569, the digit 7 stands for ⬜.

    f   In 81 465, the digit 1 stands for ⬜.

11 What does the digit **6** stand for in each of these 5-digit numbers?

    a   6 3 814   **b**   9 **6** 781   **c**   20 56 3

12 31 798 = 30 000 + 1000 + 700 + 90 + 8

              = 31 000 + 798

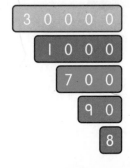  

thirty one thousand, seven hundred and ninety-eight

13 Find the missing numbers.

    a   6424 = ⬜ thousands + 4 hundreds + 2 tens + 4 ones

    b   50 328 = ⬜ + 300 + 20 + 8

14 What does the digit 5 stand for in each number?

    a   27 058   **b**   85 027   **c**   52 708

15 In 69 417, what is the value of each digit?

16 Find the missing numbers.

    a   18 294 = I ten thousand + ▢ thousands +

            2 hundreds + 9 tens + 4 ones

    b   47 093 = ▢ + 7000 + 90 + 3

Remind your child that when writing in words, it is easier to break up the number as shown: 91 485 = 91 000 + 485

                     ↑   ↑

              ninety one   four hundred and
              thousand   eighty-five

Home Maths

91 485 in words is ninety one thousand, four hundred and eighty-five. Encourage your child to use this method when writing in numbers. For example, thirty two thousand and twelve:

    a   Write the thousands in numbers: 32 000.

    b   Write the rest in numbers: 12.

    c   Add them: 32 000 + 12 = 32 012.

Game

Players: 4
You will need:
- 10 counters
- a place value chart

17 How to play:

I   Work in groups of four.
As a group, put the counters in the place value chart to make a 5-digit number.
You don't have to use all the counters.

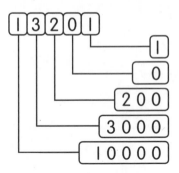

Ten Thousands	Thousands	Hundreds	Tens	Ones
●	●●●	●●		●

2   Player I writes the value of each digit in the 5-digit number like this:

3   Check the answer as a group. Player I gets I point for a correct answer.

4   As a group, rearrange the counters in the place value chart to make another 5-digit number.

5   Take turns to write the values of the digits in the number made. Play 3 rounds each.

The player with the highest score wins!

Practice Book 4A, p.9

14

Let's Learn!

Comparing numbers within 100 000

We can use place value charts to help us compare numbers.

Which number is greater, 93 085 or 76 105?

Ten Thousands	Thousands	Hundreds	Tens	Ones
9	3	0	8	5
7	6	1	0	5

Compare the ten thousands.
9 ten thousands is greater than 7 ten thousands.
93 085 is greater than 76 105.

2 Which number is smaller, 36 520 or 37 859?

Ten Thousands	Thousands	Hundreds	Tens	Ones
3	6	5	2	0
3	7	8	5	9

First compare the ten thousands.
They are the same.
Then compare the thousands.
6 thousands is smaller than 7 thousands.
36 520 is smaller than 37 859.

3 Which is greater?

    a   90 847 or 69 948   **b**   64 515 or 65 500

    c   31 256 or 31 265   **d**   19 283 or 19 289

4 Which is smaller?

    a   42 100 or 41 002   **b**   16 935 or 16 918

5 Arrange the numbers 62 357, 9638 and 28 986 in order. Begin with the greatest.

Ten Thousands	Thousands	Hundreds	Tens	Ones
6	2	3	5	7
	9	6	3	8
2	8	9	8	6

Compare the ten thousands.

6 ten thousands is greater than 0 ten thousands and 2 ten thousands.

2 ten thousands is greater than 0 ten thousands.

The numbers arranged in order, beginning with the greatest, are:

62 357, 28 986, 9638
greatest

6 Arrange the numbers in order. Begin with the smallest.

    a   9456, 73 842, 30 512

    b   41 325, 31 425, 51 324, 14 325

    c   27 084, 20 784, 27 840, 20 874

7 Look at these two numbers: 65 123 and 67 123.

Ten Thousands	Thousands	Hundreds	Tens	Ones
6	5	1	2	3
6	7	1	2	3

Compare the thousands.

65 123 is 2000 less than 67 123.

2000 more than 65 123 is ☐.

67 123 is 2000 more than 65 123.

2000 less than 67 123 is ☐.

8 Look at these two numbers: 37 625 and 7625.

Ten Thousands	Thousands	Hundreds	Tens	Ones
3	7	6	2	5
	7	6	2	5

a 30 000 more than 7625 is ☐.

b ☐ is 30 000 less than 37 625.

9 Find the missing numbers.

a 30 000 less than 34 200 is ☐.

b ☐ is 20 000 more than 53.

c 100 more than 58 967 is ☐.

10 Find the rule for each number pattern. Then complete the number pattern.

a 37 642, 57 642, ☐, 97 642

b 8500, ☐, 18 500, 23 500

c 2985, 2885, ☐, 2685, ☐, 2485

d 24 701, 26 702, 28 703, ☐, ☐

e 18 079, 20 079, 20 279, 22 279, 22 479, ☐, ☐, 26 679

Activity

11 Work in groups of four.

    1   Make four sets of number cards from 0 to 9.

    2   Shuffle the number cards.
        Take turns to pick five number cards each.

    3   Arrange your number cards to make a 5-digit number.

    4   As a group compare all four 5-digit numbers.
        Then arrange the numbers in order, beginning with the greatest.

Let's Explore!

12 Look at the numbers in the grid below.

		40 432		
		30 432		
18 432	19 432	20 432	21 432	22 432
		10 432		
		432		

    a   What do you notice about the numbers
        across the grid starting with 18 432?

    b   What do you notice about the numbers
        down the grid starting with 40 432?

    c   Look at the numbers in the green set.
        Then look at the numbers in the yellow set.
        Can you spot the similarity? What is it?

    d   Look at the numbers in the purple set.
        Then look at the numbers in the blue set.
        Can you spot the similarity? What is it?

Maths Journal

13

I Look at the four numbers: 4509   45   45009   450

What steps would you take to arrange the numbers in order, beginning with the smallest?

2 Look at the four numbers: 2137   3721   2109   3748

What steps would you take to arrange the numbers in order, beginning with the greatest?

Practice Book 4A, p.II

Put On Your Thinking Caps!

14

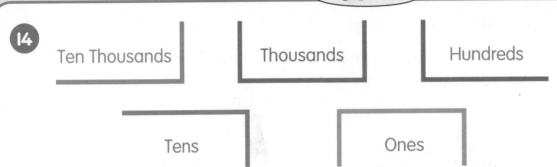

Ten Thousands   Thousands   Hundreds

Tens   Ones

Look at the pieces above. Each piece shows a place value.
Find the value of the following numbers using the pieces.

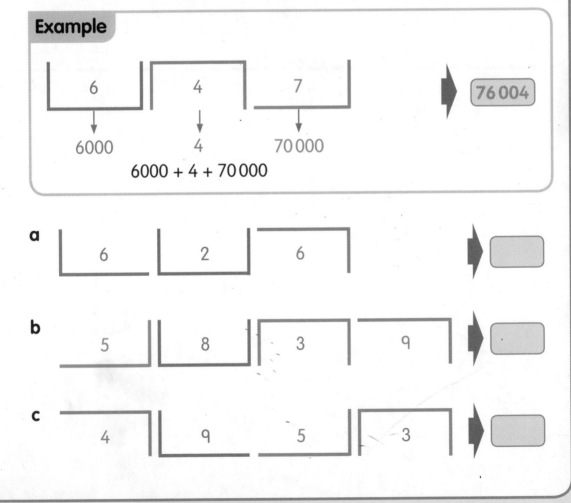

Example

6 → 6000

4 → 4

7 → 70 000

76 004

6000 + 4 + 70 000

a 6 2 6

b 5 8 3 9

c 4 9 5 3

Put On Your Thinking Caps!

15 **a** Work in pairs.

10 000   20 000

I Copy the number line.

2 Divide the number line into 10 equal parts and write the value of each part.

3 Show with arrows where to place the numbers 16 500, 19 750 and 12 000 on the number line.

(Hint: Compare 16 500, 19 750 and 12 000 with the numbers on the number line before placing them.)

b

16 500   16 600

I Copy the number line.

2 Divide the number line into 10 equal parts and write the value of each part.

3 Show with arrows where to place the numbers 16 560, 16 510 and 16 575 on the number line.

Practice Book 4A, p.15   Practice Book 4A, p.16

 **2** Whole Numbers (2)

Let's Learn!

Rounding numbers to the nearest ten

I Ribbon A is 82 cm long.

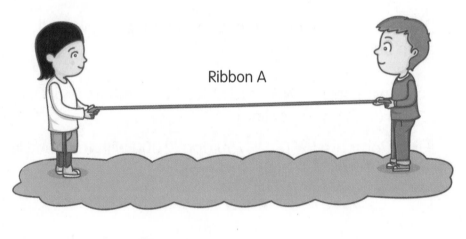

Ribbon A

82 is between 80 and 90.
It is nearer to 80 than to 90.
82 is 80 when rounded to the nearest ten.
We say 82 **is approximately equal to** 80.
We write $82 \approx 80$.

Ribbon A is 80 cm long when rounded to
the nearest ten centimetres.

We use the approximation sign $\approx$
to stand for approximately
equal to.
It shows we have rounded the
numbers.

2 Ribbon B is 17 cm long.

Ribbon B

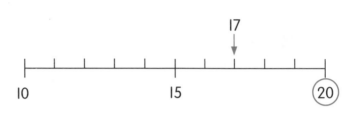

17 is between 10 and 20.

It is nearer to 20 than to 10.

17 is ⬜ when rounded to the nearest ten.

17 ≈ ⬜

Ribbon B is ⬜ cm long when rounded to the nearest ten centimetres.

3 Ribbon C is 95 cm long.

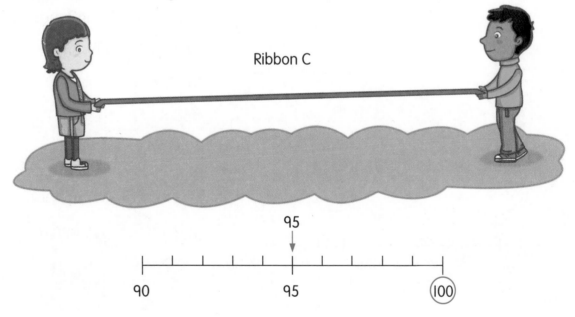

Ribbon C

95 is exactly halfway between 90 and 100.
95 is 100 when rounded to the nearest ten.
95 ≈ 100
Ribbon C is 100 cm long when rounded to the nearest ten centimetres.

4 Copy the number line shown below.
Mark each number with a cross (**X**) on the number line.
Then round the number to the nearest ten and circle it.

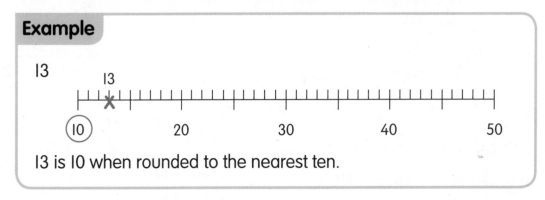

Example

13

13 is 10 when rounded to the nearest ten.

a 29 **b** 36 **c** 45 **d** 14

5 Round each number to the nearest ten.

a 42 **c** 97 **c** 25 **d** 64

6 Round 863 to the nearest ten.

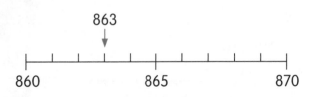

863 is between 860 and 870.

It is nearer to 860 than to 870.

863 is ⬚ when rounded to the nearest ten.

863 ≈ ⬚

7 Round 4156 to the nearest ten.

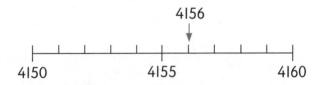

4156 is between 4150 and 4160.

It is nearer to 4160 than to 4150.

4156 is ⬚ when rounded to the nearest ten.

4156 ≈ ⬚

Home Maths

When rounding a number to the nearest ten, encourage your child to use this method: underline the digit in the tens place and circle the digit in the ones place.

50 ⟵ 5 ⑧ ⟶ 60

↑ ↑

This will tell you the nearest tens are 50 and 60. This will tell you which ten to round to.

8 Round 86 455 to the nearest ten.

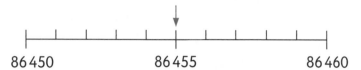

86 455 is exactly halfway between 86 450 and 86 460.

86 455 is [ ] when rounded to the nearest ten.

86 455 ≈ [ ]

9 For each number, draw a number line.
Then mark the number with a cross (**X**) on the number line.
Finally round the number to the nearest ten and circle it
on the number line.

For each number, where do I
start and end the number line?

Example

306

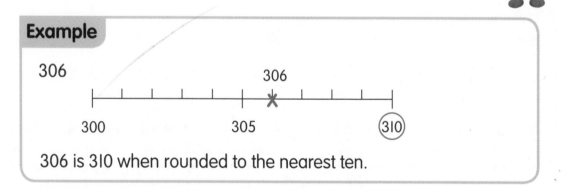

306 is 310 when rounded to the nearest ten.

Look at each number and find the nearest ten before and after it.

In the example, the number 306 lies between these two nearest tens.

300 ← nearest ten before it — 306 — nearest ten after it → 310

The number line for 306 should start at 300 and end at 310.

a 615   **b** 6381   **c** 81 098

Activity

10 Work in pairs.
Use number lines to help you.

a Find all the whole numbers that give the following answers when rounded to the nearest ten.

50 570 5000

b For each set of answers in **a**, which is

the smallest number the greatest whole number?

Example

60

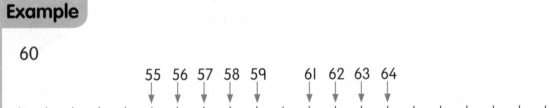

a 55, 56, 57, 58, 59, 61, 62, 63 and 64 give the answer 60 when rounded to the nearest ten.

b 55 is the smallest number. 64 is the greatest whole number.

11 Find:

a the smallest number **b** the greatest whole number

that gives 5470 when rounded to the nearest ten.

Practice Book 4A, p.17

Let's Learn!

Rounding numbers to the nearest hundred

 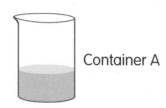

Container A

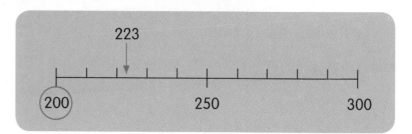

The volume of water in Container A is 223 ml.

223 is between 200 and 300.
It is nearer to 200 than to 300.
223 is 200 when rounded to the nearest hundred.
223 ≈ 200

The volume of water in Container A is 200 ml when rounded to the nearest hundred millilitres.

2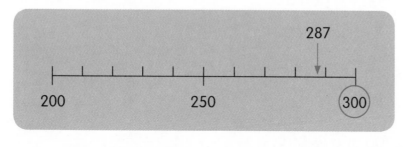

Container B

The volume of water in Container B is 287 ml.

287 is between ⬚ and 300.

It is nearer to 300 than to 200.
287 is 300 when rounded to the nearest hundred.
287 ≈ 300

The volume of water in Container B is 300 ml when rounded to the nearest hundred millilitres.

3

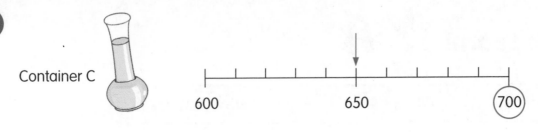

Container C

600   650   (700)

The volume of water in Container C is 650 ml.

650 is exactly halfway between 600 and 700.
650 is 700 when rounded to the nearest hundred.
650 ≈ 700

The volume of water in Container C is 700 ml when rounded to the
nearest hundred millilitres.

4 Round each of the following to the nearest hundred.

a   216   **b**   502   **c**   340   **d**   985

e   125 cm   **f**   872 kg   **g**   359 m   **h**   997 ℓ

5 Round 2372 to the nearest hundred.

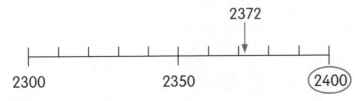

2372

2300   2350   (2400)

2372 is between 2300 and 2400.
It is nearer to 2400 than to 2300.
2372 is 2400 when rounded to the nearest hundred.
2372 ≈ 2400

6 Round 14 632 to the nearest hundred.

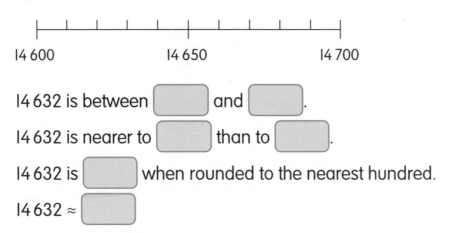

14 632 is between ☐ and ☐.

14 632 is nearer to ☐ than to ☐.

14 632 is ☐ when rounded to the nearest hundred.

14 632 ≈ ☐

7 For each number, draw a number line.
Then mark the number with a cross (**X**) on the number line.
Finally round number to the nearest hundred and circle it.

Example

68 950

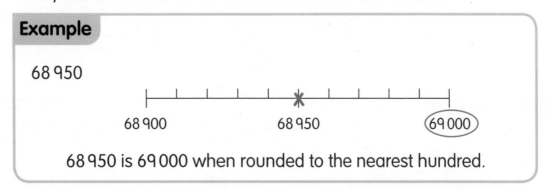

68 900   68 950   69 000

68 950 is 69 000 when rounded to the nearest hundred.

(Hint: To decide where to start and end a number line, look at each number and find the nearest hundred before and after it. In the example, the number 68 950 lies between these two nearest hundreds.

68 900 ← nearest hundred before it — 68 950 — nearest hundred after it → 69 000

So the number line for 68 950 should start at 68 900 and end at 69 000.)

a	516	b	940	c	5026
d	4158	e	62 502	f	90 048

8 Round each number to the nearest ten and hundred.

Number	Rounded to the Nearest	
	Ten	Hundred
a 68		
b 482		
c 3209		
d 14 735		

9 A number when rounded to the nearest hundred is 2800.

2700   2800   2900

a Find all the whole numbers that give 2800 when rounded to the nearest hundred. Mark these numbers with a cross (**X**) on the number line.

b Which of these is:

the smallest number?

the greatest whole number?

10 Find:

a the smallest number

b the greatest whole number

that gives 9300 when rounded to the nearest hundred.

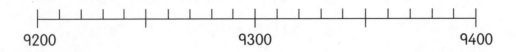

9200   9300   9400

Activity

II Work in pairs. Look at the map below.
It shows the distances between some European cities and London.

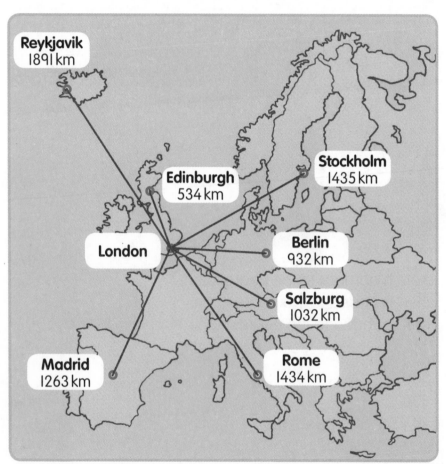

Reykjavik
1891 km

Stockholm
1435 km

Edinburgh
534 km

London

Berlin
932 km

Salzburg
1032 km

Madrid
1263 km

Rome
1434 km

Round each distance to the nearest hundred kilometres.
Write down your answers like this:

Example

The distance between London and Edinburgh
is 534 km.
534 km is 500 km when rounded to the
nearest hundred kilometres.

Practice Book 4A, p.21

Let's Learn!

Estimation

 1

$$
\begin{array}{r}
4\,7 \\
+\ 8\,1 \\
\hline
1\,2\,8
\end{array}
$$

Let's estimate the value of 47 + 81 to check the answer.

First round each number to the nearest ten.
47 is 50 when rounded to the nearest ten.
81 is 80 when rounded to the nearest ten.

$47 \approx 50$
$81 \approx 80$

Then add.
$50 + 80 = 130$
$47 + 81 \approx 130$
The value of 47 + 81 is about 130.

$128 \approx 130$
The answer is **reasonable**.

2 Estimate the value of 84 – 42.

First round each number to the nearest ten.
84 is 80 when rounded to the nearest ten.
42 is 40 when rounded to the nearest ten.

$84 \approx 80$
$42 \approx 40$

Then subtract.
$80 - 40 = 40$
$84 - 42 \approx 40$
The value of 84 – 42 is about 40.

3 Estimate the value of 64 × 3.

First round 64 to the nearest ten.
64 is 60 when rounded to the nearest ten.

Then multiply.
60 × 3 = 180
So 64 × 3 ≈ 180.
The value of 64 × 3 is about 180.

4 Estimate the value of 267 × 7.

First round 267 to the nearest hundred.

267 is ☐ when rounded to the nearest hundred.

267 ≈ ☐

Then multiply.

☐ × 7 = ☐

So 267 × 7 ≈ ☐.

The value of 267 × 7 is about ☐.

5 Estimate the value of 372 ÷ 4.
360 ◄——— 372 ———► 400

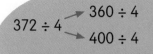
372 ÷ 4
360 ÷ 4
400 ÷ 4
372 is nearer to 360 than to 400.

Then divide.
360 ÷ 4 = 90
So 372 ÷ 4 ≈ 90.
The value of 372 ÷ 4 is about 90.

6 Estimate the value of 559 ÷ 6.

540 ◄─────── 559 ──────► 600

Then divide.

[ ] ÷ 6 = [ ]

So 559 ÷ 6 ≈ [ ].

The value of 559 ÷ 6 is about [ ].

559 ÷ 6 ➚ 540 ÷ 6
        ➘ 600 ÷ 6

559 is nearer to 540 than to 600.

7 Estimate the value of 478 ÷ 8.

[ ] ◄─────── 478 ──────► [ ]

Then divide.

[ ] ÷ 8 = [ ]

So 478 ÷ 8 ≈ [ ].

The value of 478 ÷ 8 is about [ ].

478 ÷ 8 ➚ [ ] ÷ 8
        ➘ [ ] ÷ 8

478 is nearer to [ ] than to [ ].

8 Estimate the value of 775 ÷ 8.

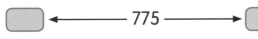

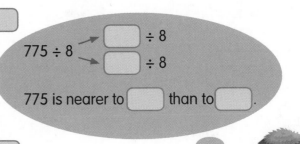

775 ÷ 8 ⟶ ☐ ÷ 8
☐ ÷ 8

775 is nearer to ☐ than to ☐.

☐ ÷ 8 = ☐

So 775 ÷ 8 ≈ ☐.

The value of 775 ÷ 8 is about ☐.

9 Round each number to the nearest ten. Then estimate the value of:

a   53 + 79

b   456 − 25

c   869 − 63

d   681 − 208

10 Round each number to the nearest hundred. Then estimate the value of:

a   634 + 512

b   2918 + 103

c   426 − 296

d   1842 − 463

11 Estimate the value of:

a   23 × 4

b   395 × 6

c   624 + 482 + 127

d   825 + 403 + 798

12 Estimate the value of:

a   92 ÷ 3

b   318 ÷ 4

13 Estimate the value of:

a   176 ÷ 5

b   640 ÷ 7

Practice Book 4A, p.25

Let's Learn!

Factors

        $1 \times 6 = 6$

Can 6 be divided exactly by 1? Yes. So 1 is a factor of 6.
Can 6 be divided exactly by 6? Yes. So 6 is a factor of 6.

6 is the **product** of 1 and 6.
1 and 6 are **factors** of 6.

$2 \times 3 = 6$ $3 \times 2 = 6$

Can 6 be divided exactly by 2?   Yes. So 2 is a factor of 6.
Can 6 be divided exactly by 3?   Yes. So 3 is also a factor of 6.
Can 6 be divided exactly by 5?   No. So 5 is not a factor of 6.
Can 6 be divided exactly by 4?   No. So 4 is not a factor of 6.

6 is the product of 2 and 3.
3 and 2 are factors of 6.
The factors of 6 are 1, 2, 3 and 6.

 Encourage your child to revise the times tables up to
12 × 12 as this will help them find the factors of a number.

3 What are the factors of 32?

$32 = 1 \times 32$
$32 = 2 \times 16$
$32 = 4 \times 8$

The factors of 32 are ⬚ , ⬚ , ⬚ , ⬚ , ⬚ and ⬚ .

4 List all the factors of 24.

$24 = $ ⬚ $\times$ ⬚

$24 = $ ⬚ $\times$ ⬚

$24 = $ ⬚ $\times$ ⬚

$24 = $ ⬚ $\times$ ⬚

The factors of 24 are ⬚ , ⬚ , ⬚ , ⬚ , ⬚ , ⬚ , ⬚ and ⬚ .

5 Is 3 a factor of 12?

```
      4
 3 ) 1 2
     1 2
    ─────
       0
```

12 can be divided exactly by 3.
So 3 is a factor of 12.

6 Is 5 a factor of 16?

```
      3
 5 ) 1 6
     1 5
    ─────
       1
```

16 cannot be divided exactly by 5.
So 5 is not a factor of 16.

7 Find the factors of:

a 12

b 28

c 56

d 100

8 What are the common factors of 8 and 12?

$$8 = 1 \times 8 \qquad 12 = 1 \times 12$$
$$8 = 2 \times 4 \qquad 12 = 2 \times 6$$
$$\qquad\qquad\quad 12 = 3 \times 4$$

The factors of 8 are (1), (2), (4) and 8.

The factors of 12 are (1), (2), 3, (4), 6 and 12.

The **common factors** of 8 and 12 are 1, 2 and 4.

9 Find the common factors of 9 and 36.

$$9 = 1 \times 9 \qquad 36 = 1 \times 36$$
$$9 = 3 \times 3 \qquad 36 = 2 \times 18$$
$$\qquad\qquad\quad 36 = 3 \times 12$$
$$\qquad\qquad\quad 36 = 4 \times 9$$
$$\qquad\qquad\quad 36 = 6 \times 6$$

The factors of 9 are ☐ , ☐ , and ☐ .

The factors of 36 are ☐ , ☐ , ☐ , ☐ , ☐ , ☐ ,
☐ , ☐ and ☐ .

The common factors of 9 and 36 are ☐ , ☐ , and ☐ .

10 Answer these questions.

a Is 5 a factor of 20?

b Is 5 a factor of 35?

c Is 5 a common factor of 20 and 35?

d Is 2 a factor of 24?

e Is 2 a factor of 27?

f Is 2 a common factor of 24 and 27?

g Is 3 a common factor of 30 and 40?

h Is 4 a common factor of 96 and 48?

II Find the common factors of:

a 32 and 12

b 12 and 16

c 60 and 54

d 45 and 96

Let's Explore!

12 Work in pairs.
Look at these numbers.

2, 5, 6, 8, 9, 11, 14, 15, 18, 20, 22, 23, 25
30, 32, 37, 38, 40, 43, 45

I Divide each number by 2. Draw the table
and write each number in the correct column.

Numbers that can be Divided Exactly by 2	Numbers that can't be Divided Exactly by 2

> When a number can be divided exactly by another number, there is no remainder.

a What do you notice about the numbers in the column
on the left compared to those in the column on the right?

b What can you say about all the numbers which can be
divided exactly by 2?

Let's Explore!

2 Look at the numbers again. Divide each number by 5. Draw the table and write each number in the correct column.

Numbers that can be Divided Exactly by 5	Numbers that can't be Divided Exactly by 5

a What do you notice about the numbers in the column on the left compared to those in the column on the right?

b What can you say about all the numbers which can be divided exactly by 5?

Maths Journal

13 **a** These are the steps to find the factors of the number 12.

Think of all the numbers that 12 can be divided by without a remainder.

$12 \div 1 = 12$ $12 \div 4 = 3$

$12 \div 2 = 6$ $12 \div 6 = 2$

$12 \div 3 = 4$ $12 \div 12 = 1$

Think of the times tables.
$12 = 1 \times 12$
$12 = 2 \times 6$
$12 = 3 \times 4$

The factors are 1, 2, 3, 4, 6 and 12.

b Write down the steps for finding the common factors of 12 and 15.

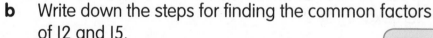

Practice Book 4A, p.27

Let's Learn!

Multiples

1 What are the multiples of 3?

> Here is the 3 times table:
> $1 \times 3 = \mathbf{3}$, $\quad 2 \times 3 = \mathbf{6}$, $\quad 3 \times 3 = \mathbf{9}$,
> $4 \times 3 = \mathbf{12}$, $\quad 5 \times 3 = \mathbf{15}$, $\quad 6 \times 3 = \mathbf{18}$,
> $7 \times 3 = \mathbf{21}$, $\quad 8 \times 3 = \mathbf{24}$, $\quad 9 \times 3 = \mathbf{27}$,
> $10 \times 3 = \mathbf{30}$, $\quad 11 \times 3 = \mathbf{33}$, $\quad 12 \times 3 = \mathbf{36}$

3, 6, 9, 12, 15, 18, 21, 24, 27, 30, 33 and 36 are **multiples** of 3 because they are all in the 3 times table.

2 Is 12 a multiple of 3? Yes.

```
      4
3 ) 1 2
    1 2
    ___
      0
```

> 12 can be divided exactly by 3.
> 12 is a multiple of 3.
> 3 is a factor of 12.

Is 28 a multiple of 3? No.

```
      9
3 ) 2 8
    2 7
    ___
      1
```

> 28 cannot be divided exactly by 3.
> 28 is not a multiple of 3.
> 3 is not a factor of 28.

> 3 is a factor of all multiples of 3.

3 Answer these questions.

    a Is 24 a multiple of 8?

    b Is 42 a multiple of 5?

4 What are the first three multiples of 7?

> Here is the 7 times table:
> $1 \times 7 = 7$, $2 \times 7 = 14$, $3 \times 7 = 21$,
> $4 \times 7 = 28$, $5 \times 7 = 35$, $6 \times 7 = 42$,
> $7 \times 7 = 49$, $8 \times 7 = 56$, $9 \times 7 = 63$,
> $10 \times 7 = 70$, $11 \times 7 = 77$, $12 \times 7 = 84$

7, 14, 21, 28 ..., 84 are multiples of 7.

The **first multiple** of 7 is 7.
The **second multiple** of 7 is 14.
The **third multiple** of 7 is 21.

> 7 is a factor of all multiples of 7.
>
> 7 is a factor of 7.
> 7 is a factor of 14.
> 7 is a factor of 21.

5 Answer these questions.

a What is the fourth multiple of 7?

b What is the fifth multiple of 7?

c What is the twelfth multiple of 7?

6 Find the first five multiples of each number.

a 2   **b** 10

c 6   **d** 8

7 What is a common multiple of 3 and 5?

> $3 \times 1 = 3$ $5 \times 1 = 5$
> $3 \times 2 = 6$ $5 \times 2 = 10$
> $3 \times 3 = 9$ $5 \times 3 = 15$
> $3 \times 4 = 12$ $5 \times 4 = 20$
> $3 \times 5 = 15$ $5 \times 5 = 25$

The multiples of 3 are 3, 6, 9, 12, ⑮ ...

The multiples of 5 are 5, 10, ⑮, 20, 25...

A **common multiple** of 3 and 5 is 15.

8 List the first twelve multiples of 4 and 6.
Which of these are common multiples of 4 and 6?

The first twelve multiples of 4 are [ ], [ ], [ ], [ ], [ ], [ ],
[ ], [ ], [ ], [ ], [ ] and [ ].

The first twelve multiples of 6 are [ ], [ ], [ ], [ ], [ ], [ ],
[ ], [ ], [ ], [ ], [ ] and [ ].

From the list of twelve multiples, the common multiples of 4 and 6 are

[ ].

9 Find a common multiple of:

a 3 and 4 **b** 5 and 4 **c** 2 and 7

10 List the first twelve multiples of 5 and 8. Which of these is a common
multiple of 5 and 8?

11 15 and 30 are common multiples of 5 and X. X is a one-digit number and
it is not 1. What is this number X?

Practice Book 4A, p.29

Put On Your Thinking Caps!

12 Mrs Brook wrote a number on a card without showing the card to her class.
She asked her class what the number was. She gave them three hints.

- The number can be divided exactly by 3.
- When I add 3 to the number, it can be divided exactly by 5.
- The number is smaller than 32 but bigger than 23.

What is the number?
(Hint: First make a list of the multiples of 3 and the multiples of 5.)

13 Jack bought an item that was less than £100. He could pay for the item exactly with only £2 coins. He could also pay for the item exactly with only £5 notes. What were the likely prices of the item he bought?

14 A farmer has a rectangular field. The length of the field is five times its width. The length and width are whole numbers. The perimeter of the field is 50 m when rounded to the nearest ten metres. What are the width and length of the field?

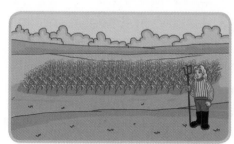

Record your answers in a table like this:

Width	Length	Perimeter	Perimeter When Rounded to The Nearest 10 m
1st guess: 1 m	5 m	1 + 1 + 5 + 5 = 12 m	10 m
2nd guess:			

Practice Book 4A, p.32   Practice Book 4A, p.34

Whole Numbers (3)

Let's Learn!

Multiplication by a 1-digit number

1   Jenny sells 2476 oranges. Mark sells 3 times as many oranges as Jenny.
How many oranges does Mark sell?

$2476 \times 3 = ?$

Step 1

Multiply 6 ones by 3.
6 ones × 3 = 18 ones
        = 1 ten 8 ones

```
  Th H T O
   2 4 7 6
 ×       3
 ─────────
         8
 ─────────
         1
```

Step 2

Multiply 7 tens by 3.
7 tens × 3 = 21 tens
        = 2 hundreds 1 ten
Add 1 ten.
2 hundreds 1 ten + 1 ten = 2 hundreds 2 tens

```
   2 4 7 6
 ×       3
 ─────────
       2 8
 ─────────
       2 1
```

Step 3

Multiply 4 hundreds by 3.
4 hundreds × 3 = 12 hundreds
           = 1 thousand 2 hundreds
Add 2 hundreds.
1 thousand 2 hundreds + 2 hundreds
= 1 thousand 4 hundreds

```
   2 4 7 6
 ×       3
 ─────────
     4 2 8
 ─────────
     1 2 1
```

Step 4

Multiply 2 thousands by 3.
2 thousands × 3 = 6 thousands
Add 1 thousand.
6 thousands + 1 thousand = 7 thousands

```
   2 4 7 6
 ×       3
 ─────────
   7 4 2 8
 ─────────
     1 2 1
```

Mark sells 7428 oranges.

2 The next month, Jenny sells 6139 oranges. Mark sells 9 times as many oranges as Jenny. How many oranges does Mark sell?

$6139 \times 9 = ?$

Th H T O

Step 1

9 ones × 9 = 81 ones

= ☐ tens ☐ one

```
    6 1 3 9
  ×       9
          1
        8
```

Step 2

3 tens × 9 = 27 tens

= ☐ hundreds ☐ tens

☐ hundreds ☐ tens + ☐ tens

= ☐ hundreds ☐ tens

= ☐ hundreds ☐ tens

```
    6 1 3 9
  ×       9
        5 1
      3 8
```

Step 3

1 hundred × 9 = 9 hundreds

☐ hundreds + ☐ hundreds

= ☐ hundreds

= ☐ thousand ☐ hundreds

```
    6 1 3 9
  ×       9
      2 5 1
    1 3 8
```

Step 4

6 thousands × 9 = 54 thousands

☐ thousands + ☐ thousand

= ☐ thousands

```
    6 1 3 9
  ×       9
  5 5 2 5 1
    1 3 8
```

Mark sells 55 251 oranges.

3 Multiply.

a
```
    1 0 2 6
×         4
```

b
```
    1 2 7 8
×         7
```

c
```
    4 6 1 6
×         5
```

4 2147 × 4 = ⬚

```
    2 1 4 7
×         4
        2 8  ←——— 7 × 4
      1 6 0  ←——— 40 × 4
      4 0 0  ←——— 100 × 4
×   8 0 0 0  ←——— 2000 × 4
    8 5 8 8
```

Here's another way to multiply.

5 Multiply using the method shown in **4**.

a
```
    6 1 7 4
×         5
```

b
```
    8 0 1 2
×         9
```

c
```
    9 0 0 9
×         9
```

Game

Players: 2
You will need:
• a 10-sided dice

6 How to play:

1 Player 1 rolls the dice four times and makes a 4-digit number, for example 7621.

2 Player 2 rolls the dice once to get a 1-digit number, for example 6.

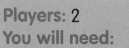
```
        7 6 2 1
×             6
      4 5 7 2 6
        3 1
```

3 Player 1 uses the method shown in **1** to multiply the 4-digit number by the 1-digit number.

Game

4 Player I writes down the answer like this:

Example

4-digit Number	I-digit Number	Product
7621	6	7621 × 6 = 45 726

5 Player 2 checks the answer. Player I gets I point if the answer is correct.

The player with the highest score wins!

6 Take turns to play. Play three rounds.

7 Estimate the value of 2178 × 3.

2000   2500   3000

2178 is nearer to 2000 than to 3000.

$2178 \times 3 \approx 2000 \times 3$
$= 6000$
So $2178 \times 3 \approx 6000$.

8 Estimate the value of 7650 × 4.

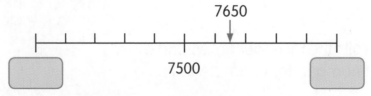

7500

7650 is nearer to ☐ than to ☐.

$7650 \times 4 \approx$ ☐ $\times 4$

$=$ ☐

So $7650 \times 4 \approx$ ☐.

9 Calculate 3167 × 3. Estimate to check whether your answer is reasonable.

Calculation:

```
    3 1 6 7
  ×       3
  ─────────
    9 5 0 1
    ─────────
      2 2
```

Estimation:

```
    3 0 0 0
  ×       3
  ─────────
    9 0 0 0
```

The estimated value 9000 is close to the actual value 9501. The answer 9501 is reasonable.

10 Calculate 4943 × 5. Estimate to check whether your answer is reasonable.

Calculation:

```
    4 9 4 3
  ×       5
  ─────────
  [      ]
```

Estimation:

```
  [        ]
  ×       5
  ─────────
  [        ]
```

Is your actual answer reasonable? Why?

Let's Explore!

11 Look at how these questions have been worked out and their answers. What is wrong with each of them?

Talk with your classmates and identify mistakes that pupils make when doing multiplication calculations.

a
```
    1 2 4 5
  ×       8
  ─────────
    8 6 2 0
    ─────────
    1 3   4
```

b
```
      6 7 3
  ×       3
  ─────────
  1 8 2 1 9
```

c
```
    1 0 3 6
  ×       5
  ─────────
    5 5 8 0
    ─────────
    1   3
```

> Practice Book 4A, p.39

Let's Learn!

Multiplication by a 2-digit number

1 Paul packs 4 bags of apples. Each bag contains 10 apples. How many apples does Paul pack altogether?

$4 \times 10 = 4 \times 1$ ten
$\qquad = 4$ tens
$\qquad = 40$

1 ten = 10
10 = 1 ten
40 = 4 tens

Paul packs 40 apples altogether.

2 A greengrocer buys 3 boxes of bananas. Each box contains 20 bananas. How many bananas does the greengrocer buy?

$3 \times 20 = 3 \times 2$ tens
$\qquad = 6$ tens
$\qquad = 60$

2 tens = 20
20 = 2 tens

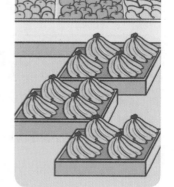

The greengrocer buys 60 bananas.

3 Find the missing numbers.

a $\quad 14 \times 10 = \boxed{} \times \boxed{}$ ten $= \boxed{}$ tens $= \boxed{}$

b $\quad 7 \times 30 = \boxed{} \times \boxed{}$ tens $= \boxed{}$ tens $= \boxed{}$

c $\quad 58 \times 60 = \boxed{} \times \boxed{}$ tens $= \boxed{}$ tens $= \boxed{}$

4 Find the missing numbers.

a $9 \times 40 = 9 \times$ ⬜ tens = ⬜ tens = ⬜

b $47 \times 80 =$ ⬜ $\times$ ⬜ tens = ⬜ tens = ⬜

5 Find the product of 24 and 30.

Method I

$$24 \times 30 = 24 \times 3 \times 10$$
$$= 72 \times 10$$
$$= 720$$

$30 = 3 \times 10$

Method 2

$$24 \times 30 = 24 \times 10 \times 3$$
$$= 240 \times 3$$
$$= 720$$

$30 = 10 \times 3$

6 Find the missing numbers.

a $37 \times 20 = 37 \times$ ⬜ $\times 10 =$ ⬜ $\times 10 =$ ⬜

b $43 \times 50 = 43 \times$ ⬜ $\times 5 =$ ⬜ $\times 5 =$ ⬜

c $216 \times 30 = 216 \times$ ⬜ $\times 10 =$ ⬜ $\times 10 =$ ⬜

d $754 \times 80 = 754 \times$ ⬜ $\times 8 =$ ⬜ $\times 8 =$ ⬜

7 Multiply.

a 32×10 b 93×30 c 41×50

d 68×80 e 457×10 f 210×20

g 831×40 h 379×70

8 A ship carries petrol in 27 barrels. Each barrel contains 32 litres of petrol. What is the total volume of petrol carried on the ship?

27 × 32 = ?

Step 1

Multiply 2 tens 7 ones by 2.
7 ones × 2 = 14 ones
        = 1 ten 4 ones
2 tens × 2 = 4 tens
Add.
4 tens + 1 ten 4 ones = 5 tens 4 ones
27 × 2 = 54

```
      1
    2 7
  ×  3 2
  ─────────
    5 4
  ─────────
```

Step 2

Multiply 2 tens 7 ones by 30.
7 ones × 30 = 210 ones
           = 21 tens
           = 2 hundreds 1 ten
2 tens × 30 = 60 tens
           = 6 hundreds
Add.
6 hundreds + 2 hundreds 1 ten
= 8 hundreds 1 ten
27 × 30 = 810

```
      2
      1
    2 7
  ×  3 2
  ─────────
    5 4
  8 1 0
  ─────────
```

Step 3

Add.
54 + 810 = 864
27 × 32 = 864

```
      2
      1
    2 7
  ×  3 2
  ─────────
    5 4
  8 1 0
  ─────────
  8 6 4
```

The ship carries 864 litres of petrol.

9 Find the product.

a
```
      4 6
  ×   5 8
  ─────────
```

b
```
      6 2
  ×   1 5
  ─────────
```

c
```
      8 7
  ×   3 5
  ─────────
```

10 A plant needs 315 ml water a week. How much water does it need in 23 weeks?

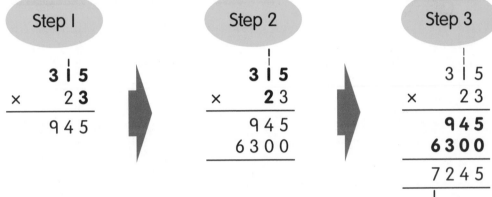

Step 1	Step 2	Step 3
3 1 5 × 2 3 ───── 9 4 5	3 1 5 × 2 3 ───── 9 4 5 6 3 0 0	3 1 5 × 2 3 ───── **9 4 5** **6 3 0 0** ───── 7 2 4 5

The plant needs 7245 ml in 23 weeks.

11 Multiply.

a
```
    3 7 9
  ×   2 2
  ─────────
```

b
```
    7 8 5
  ×   1 7
  ─────────
```

c
```
    9 3 7
  ×   1 6
  ─────────
```

d
```
    6 0 5
  ×   4 8
  ─────────
```

e
```
    7 0 0
  ×   5 1
  ─────────
```

f
```
    8 0 0
  ×   6 9
  ─────────
```

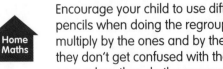

Game

Players: 2

12 How to play:

1 Each player writes a multiplication question:
2-digit number × 2-digit number.

Example

```
      4 3
  ×   3 5
  ───────
    2 1 5
  1 2 9 0
  ───────
  1 5 0 5
```

2 Each player works out the answer. Then they replace any 3 numbers in their working with boxes.

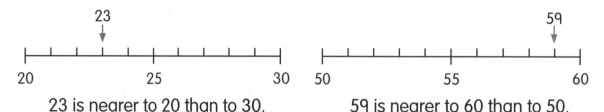

```
      4 3
  ×   3 5
  ───────
  ☐ 1  5
  1 2 ☐ 0   } working
  ───────
  1 ☐ 0  5
```

3 Players exchange questions and fill in the missing numbers.

. . . .
The first player to fill in the boxes
with the correct numbers wins!
. . . .

13 Estimate the value of 23 × 59.

23 →
```
├──┼──┼──┼──┼──┼──┼──┼──┼──┤
20          25          30
```
23 is nearer to 20 than to 30.

59 →
```
├──┼──┼──┼──┼──┼──┼──┼──┼──┤
50          55          60
```
59 is nearer to 60 than to 50.

23 × 59 ≈ 20 × 60
        = 1200

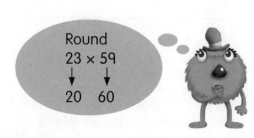

Round
23 × 59
↓   ↓
20 60

14 Estimate the value of 38 × 715.

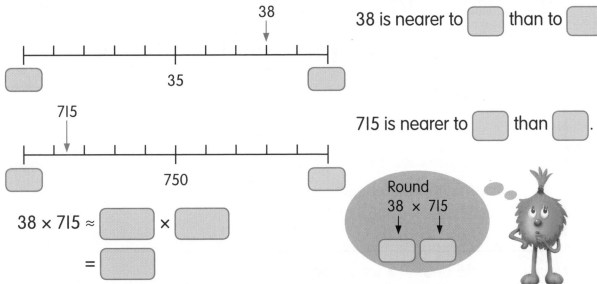

38 is nearer to ☐ than to ☐.

715 is nearer to ☐ than ☐.

$38 \times 715 \approx$ ☐ × ☐

= ☐

Round
38 × 715
↓ ↓
☐ ☐

15 Calculate. Then estimate to check whether your answer is reasonable.

a   68 × 94

b   489 × 27

Let's Explore!

16 For each of the following questions, spot the mistakes and work out the answer.

a
```
      2 5 9
  ×     6 2
  ─────────
      4 1 8
  1 2 5 4 0
  ─────────
  1 2 9 5 8
```

b
```
        5 7
  ×     3 3
  ─────────
      1 7 1
      1 7 1
  ─────────
      3 4 2
```

c
```
      3 6 5
  ×     8 6
  ─────────
  2 1 9 0
  2 9 5 0
  ─────────
  5 1 4 0
```

Talk with your classmates and identify mistakes that pupils make when doing multiplication calculations.

Maths Journal

17 Look at the steps for multiplying a 3-digit number by a 1-digit number.

$$
\begin{array}{r}
2\ 1\ 5 \\
\times \qquad 7 \\
\hline
1\ 5\ 0\ 5 \\
\end{array}
$$

1   3

1 Multiply the ones by 7.
5 ones × 7 = 35 ones

2 Regroup the ones.
35 ones = 3 tens **5 ones**

3 Multiply the ten by 7.
1 ten × 7 = 7 tens

4 Add the tens.
7 tens + 3 tens = 10 tens

5 Regroup the tens.
10 tens = 1 hundred **0 tens**

6 Multiply the hundreds by 7.
2 hundreds × 7 = 14 hundreds

7 Add the hundreds.
14 hundreds + 1 hundred = 15 hundreds

8 Regroup the hundreds.
15 hundreds = **1 thousand 5 hundreds**

9 The product is **1505**.

18 What are the steps to multiply 6875 × 3?

Practice Book 4A, p.43

Let's Learn!

Division by a 1-digit number

1 6381 seeds are planted in plant pots. Each plant pot contains 3 seeds. How many plant pots are there?

Th H T O

Step 1

Divide 6 thousands by 3.

```
      2
3 ) 6  3  8  1
    6          ← 2 × 3
```

6 thousands ÷ 3 = 2 thousands
= 2000

Step 2

Divide 3 hundreds by 3.

```
      2  1
3 ) 6  3  8  1
    6
    ─────
       3
       3      ← 1 × 3
```

3 hundreds ÷ 3 = 1 hundred
= 100

Step 3

Divide 8 tens by 3.

```
      2  1  2
3 ) 6  3  8  1
    6
    ───
       3
       3
    ──────
          8
          6   ← 2 × 3
       ─────
          2
```

8 tens ÷ 3 = 2 tens with remainder 2 tens
= 20 with remainder 20

Step 4

Divide 21 ones by 3.

```
      2  1  2  7
3 ) 6  3  8  1
    6
    ───
       3
       3
    ──────
          8
          6
       ─────
          2  1
          2  1  ← 7 × 3
       ───────
             0
```

21 ones ÷ 3 = 7 ones
= 7

When 6381 is divided by 3, the quotient is 2127 and the remainder is 0.
There are 2127 plant pots.

2 Divide 6144 by 6.

Th H T O

Step 1

Divide 6 thousands by 6.

$$6 \text{ thousands} \div 6 = \boxed{} \text{ thousand}$$
$$= \boxed{}$$

```
     Th H T O
  6 ) 6  1 4 4
      6
```

Step 2

Divide 1 hundred by 6.

$$1 \text{ hundred} \div 6 = \boxed{} \text{ hundred with}$$
$$\text{remainder } \boxed{} \text{ hundred}$$
$$= \boxed{} \text{ with remainder } \boxed{}$$

```
  6 ) 6  1 4 4
      6
      1
```

Step 3

Divide 14 tens by 6.

$$14 \text{ tens} \div 6 = \boxed{} \text{ tens with}$$
$$\text{remainder } \boxed{} \text{ tens}$$
$$= \boxed{} \text{ with remainder } \boxed{}$$

```
  6 ) 6  1 4 4
      6
        1 4
        1 2
          2
```

Step 4

Divide 24 ones by 6.

$$24 \text{ ones} \div 6 = \boxed{} \text{ ones}$$
$$= \boxed{}$$

When 6144 is divided by 6, the quotient
is $\boxed{}$ and the remainder is $\boxed{}$.

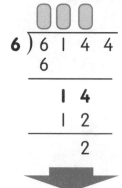

```
  6 ) 6  1 4 4
      6
        1 4
        1 2
          2 4
          2 4
            0
```

3 Divide.

a $6 \overline{)\, 1536}$

b $4 \overline{)\, 8216}$

4 Divide 2634 by 4. Then find the quotient and the remainder.

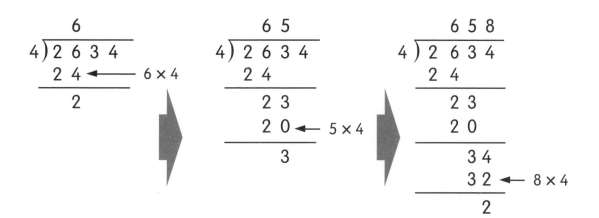

```
      6
 4)2 6 3 4
   2 4  ←——— 6 × 4
   ———
     2
```

```
      6 5
 4)2 6 3 4
   2 4
   ———
     2 3
     2 0  ←— 5 × 4
     ———
       3
```

```
      6 5 8
 4)2 6 3 4
   2 4
   ———
     2 3
     2 0
     ———
       3 4
       3 2  ←— 8 × 4
       ———
         2
```

When 2634 is divided by 4, the quotient is ⬚

and the remainder is ⬚.

5 Divide 6100 by 8. Then find the quotient and the remainder.

```
      ▢
 8)6 1 0 0
   5 6
   ———
     5
```

```
      ▢▢
 8)6 1 0 0
   5 6
   ———
     5 0
     4 8
     ———
       2
```

```
      ▢▢▢
 8)6 1 0 0
   5 6
   ———
     5 0
     4 8
     ———
       2 0
       1 6
       ———
         ▢
```

When 6100 is divided by 8, the quotient is ⬚

and the remainder is ⬚.

6 Find the quotient (q) and the remainder (r).

a 5608 ÷ 6

q = ☐ r = ☐

b 2117 ÷ 7

q = ☐ r = ☐

c 4135 ÷ 3

q = ☐ r = ☐

7 Find the quotient (q) and the remainder (r).

a 4165 ÷ 5

q = ☐ r = ☐

b 3796 ÷ 9

q = ☐ r = ☐

8 Find the quotient and the remainder.

☐

a 4)423

☐

b 9)1803

9 Estimate the value of the quotient.

a 83 ÷ 2 ≈ ☐ ÷ 2

= ☐

b 96 ÷ 5 ≈ ☐ ÷ 5

= ☐

c 865 ÷ 3 ≈ ☐ ÷ 3

= ☐

d 586 ÷ 6 ≈ ☐ ÷ 6

= ☐

e 269 ÷ 6 ≈ ☐ ÷ 6

= ☐

f 2079 ÷ 7 ≈ ☐ ÷ 7

= ☐

30 tens ÷ 6
= 5 tens
= 50

21 hundreds ÷ 7
= 3 hundreds
= 300

10 Estimate the value of the quotient.

a $764 \div 8 \approx \boxed{} \div 8$

$= \boxed{}$

b $7175 \div 9 \approx \boxed{} \div 9$

$= \boxed{}$

11 Estimate the value of the quotient.

a $47 \div 5 \approx \boxed{} \div 5$

$= \boxed{}$

b $383 \div 4 \approx \boxed{} \div 4$

$= \boxed{}$

c $617 \div 6 \approx \boxed{} \div 6$

$= \boxed{}$

d $3555 \div 9 \approx \boxed{} \div 9$

$= \boxed{}$

12 **a** Calculate $7146 \div 7$. Estimate whether your answer is reasonable.

Calculation:

$$7 \overline{)\ 7146}$$

Estimation:

$$7 \overline{)}$$

Is your actual answer reasonable?

b Calculate $6351 \div 8$. Estimate whether your answer is reasonable.

Calculation:

$$8 \overline{)\ 6351}$$

Estimation:

Is your actual answer reasonable?

13 **a** Calculate 617 ÷ 6. Estimate whether your answer is reasonable.

b Calculate 6369 ÷ 8. Estimate whether your answer is reasonable.

c Calculate 5058 ÷ 5. Estimate whether your answer is reasonable.

d Calculate 6702 ÷ 7. Estimate whether your answer is reasonable.

Let's Explore!

14 Four children, Abby, Ben, Ahmed and Chantal, answered the following question.

Estimate the value of the quotient: 468 ÷ 5

These are their answers.

Abby   2500
Ben   450
Ahmed   90
Chantal   9

Discuss with your friends how the children got their answers. Explain which three answers are not reasonable.

Practice Book 4A, p.47

Home Maths

Think of situations which will help your child to divide. For example, ask your child to help you to divide 1000 g of rice or pasta into 4 portions. Ask them to divide to find the mass of each portion and measure the portions using a kitchen scale.

Let's Learn!

Word problems

1 Mrs Elliott and Mr Smith have £4686 altogether. Mrs Elliott's share is twice as much as Mr Smith's.

   a How much is Mr Smith's share?

   b How much is Mrs Elliott's share?

   c If Mrs Elliott spends £500 on a holiday, how much money does she have left?

a   Mrs Elliott

        Mr Smith   } £4686

$$
\begin{array}{r}
1562 \\
3\,\overline{)4686} \\
3 \\
\hline
16 \\
15 \\
\hline
18 \\
18 \\
\hline
6 \\
6 \\
\hline
0 \\
\end{array}
$$

£4686 ÷ 3 = £1562

Mr Smith's share is £1562.

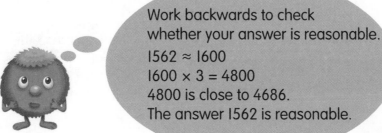

Work backwards to check whether your answer is reasonable.
1562 ≈ 1600
1600 × 3 = 4800
4800 is close to 4686.
The answer 1562 is reasonable.

b £1562 × 2 = £ ☐

   Mrs Elliott's share is £ ☐ .

$$
\begin{array}{r}
1562 \\
\times 2 \\
\hline
3124 \\
11 \\
\end{array}
$$

1562 ≈ 1600
1600 × 2 = 3200
3200 is close to 3124.
The answer is reasonable.

c £3124 − £ ☐ = £ ☐

   Mrs Elliott has £ ☐ left.

2 A youth group had £3756 for a camping trip. They saved £650 and spent the rest on 12 tents and some food for the trip. The tents cost £205 each. How much did they spend on food?

First find the total amount the youth group spent.

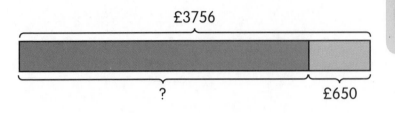

£3756

?   £650

$3756 - 650 = 3106$
They spent £3106 altogether.

£205

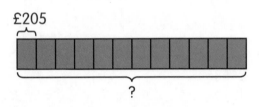

?

Next find the total cost of 12 tents.

$12 \times £205 = £\boxed{}$

The 12 tents cost £$\boxed{}$.

£3106

£$\boxed{}$?

Finally subtract the cost of 12 tents from the total amount that the youth group spent.

$£3106 - £\boxed{} = £\boxed{}$

They spent £$\boxed{}$ on food.

Home Maths Encourage your child to form a habit of checking answers to ensure they are reasonable.
Go through the problem on page 63 with them and point out that
(a) rounding and estimating answers   (b) working backwards
are useful methods for checking if answers are reasonable.

3 Sophie had 1750 football stickers. Harry had 480 fewer football stickers than Sophie. Sophie gave some football stickers to Harry. In the end, Harry had 3 times as many football stickers as Sophie.

    a How many football stickers did Harry have to begin with?

    b How many football stickers did Sophie have in the end?

a

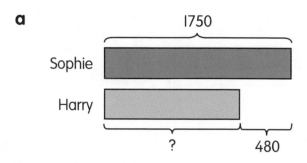

1750 − 480 = 1270

Harry had 1270 football stickers to begin with.

b 1750 + 1270 = 3020

Find the total number of football stickers Sophie and Harry had to begin with.

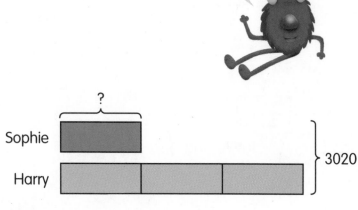

3020 ÷ 4 = 755

Sophie had 755 football stickers in the end.

4 Mr Smith has £1240 and Miss Brook has £4730.
Miss Brook gives some money to Mr Smith.
In the end, Mr Smith has twice as much money as Miss Brook.

    a   How much money does Miss Brook have in the end?

    b   How much money does Miss Brook give to Mr Smith?

a

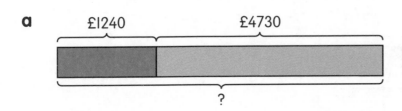

£1240   £4730

?

> First find the total sum of money Mr Smith and Miss Brook have.

£ ☐ + £ ☐ = £ ☐

Mr Smith and Miss Brook have £ ☐ altogether.

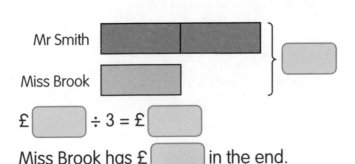

Mr Smith

Miss Brook

£ ☐ ÷ 3 = £ ☐

Miss Brook has £ ☐ in the end.

b   £4730 − £ ☐ = £ ☐

     Miss Brook gives £ ☐ to Mr Smith.

Home Maths For word problems with more than one step, encourage your child to show how to check that the answers are reasonable at each step.

5 Michael and Alisha have 96 marbles altogether. Michael loses 24 marbles to Alisha during a game. At the end of the game, Alisha has twice as many marbles as Michael. How many marbles did Alisha have to begin with?

After the game:

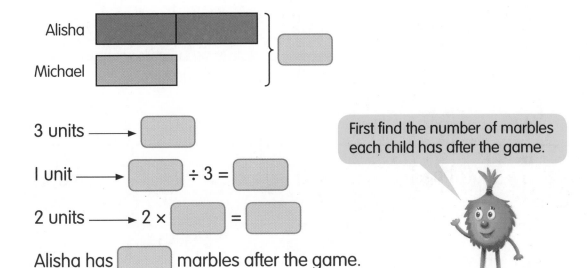

3 units ⟶ ⬚

1 unit ⟶ ⬚ ÷ 3 = ⬚

2 units ⟶ 2 × ⬚ = ⬚

Alisha has ⬚ marbles after the game.

First find the number of marbles each child has after the game.

Before the game:

⬚ – 24 = ⬚

Alisha had ⬚ marbles to begin with.

67

Activity

6 Write multiplication word problems using the words and numbers given. Then solve them.

a

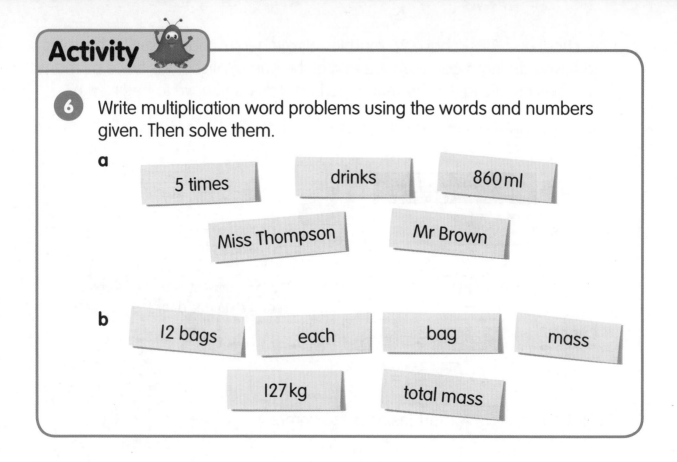

5 times   drinks   860 ml

Miss Thompson   Mr Brown

b

12 bags   each   bag   mass

127 kg   total mass

7 A shopkeeper buys 1257 tins of paint. Each tin holds 7 ℓ of paint. If he sells 620 tins, how much paint does he have left? Give your answer in litres.

8 A gardener packs 4568 seeds equally into 9 packets. He packs the greatest possible number of seeds equally and plants any remaining seeds in his own garden.

a   How many seeds are there in each packet?

b   How many seeds does he plant?

c   If he sells 7 packets, how many seeds does he have left?

9 Jack, Tai and Millie sell some raffle tickets for charity. Jack sells 125 tickets. Tai sells 14 times as many tickets as Jack. Millie sells half as many tickets as Tai. How many tickets do they sell altogether?

10 Liam runs round a rectangular field 4 times a week. The field is 320 m long and 240 m wide. Each time, he runs 6 laps. How far does he run in a week?

11 Mr Khan had 2740 g of flour at first. Mr Cook had 3560 g of flour at first. Mr Khan gave some flour to Mr Cook. In the end, Mr Cook had 4 times as much flour as Mr Khan.

   a How many grams of flour did Mr Khan have in the end?

   b How many grams of flour did Mr Cook have in the end?

12 Mrs Clark has two bank accounts, Account A and Account B. She had £2370 in Account B. She had a total of £7480 in Account A and Account B. She transferred some money from Account B to Account A. In the end, the amount of money in Account A is 3 times as much as the amount of money in Account B.

   a How much money is there in Account A in the end?

   b How much money did Mrs Clark transfer from Account B to Account A?

Let's Explore!

13 Mr Barker and Mrs Green often meet each other in a supermarket. Mr Barker goes to the supermarket every 2 days and Mrs Green goes to the supermarket every 3 days. They meet at the supermarket on 1st January. List four dates on which they will meet again in the supermarket.

(Hint: Use a calendar to help you identify the days.)

Look at the dates on which they will meet at the supermarket. Do you notice a pattern?
Based on the pattern, list another four dates on which they will meet again in the supermarket.

Practice Book 4A, p.51

Put On Your Thinking Caps!

14 a

| 12 | 865 | 470 | 45 |

Which two of the above numbers give the following products?
(Hint: Estimate to help you.)

540   5640   38 925

b   At a football match, the number of men is
3 times the number of women. The number
of women is 5 times the number of
children at the football match.

How many times the number of children is the number of men?

If there are 730 children, how many men are there?

c   A farmer puts 4 fence posts along the width of a rectangular field
as shown. The space between 2 posts is 125 cm.
If he puts posts along the length in a similar way, there will
be 10 posts. What is the perimeter of the field?

} 125 cm

Practice Book 4A, p.55   Practice Book 4A, p.56

70

Tables and Line Graphs

Let's Learn!

Presenting and interpreting data in a table

1 These cards show the names and months of the birthdays of some children.

Name: **Ella**
Month of Birthday:
March

Name: **Jack**
Month of Birthday:
May

Name: **Hardeep**
Month of Birthday:
January

Name: **Millie**
Month of Birthday:
December

Name: **Farha**
Month of Birthday:
August

Name: **Peter**
Month of Birthday:
May

The data is presented using a table like this:

Names		Months of Birthdays
	Ella	March
	Jack	May
	Hardeep	January
	Millie	December
	Farha	August
	Peter	May

a Farha's birthday is in the month of [ ].

b [ ] birthday is in the month of December.

c Two children were born in the month of [ ].

d If all of them were born in the same year,

   i   who is the youngest?

   ii   who is the oldest?

   iii   who is younger than Ella?

   iv   who is older than Ella?

2 Miss Jones asks each child to bring one type of food for a picnic. At the picnic, she counts the number of each type of food brought.

Sandwich	Apple	Orange	Cheese twist	Others
IIII	TₕₗL	TₕₗL II	III	TₕₗL

Miss Jones adds the tallies to find the number of children who have brought each type of food. Then she presents her data in a table like this:

Types of Food	Sandwich	Apple	Orange	Cheese twist	Others
Number of Children	4	5	7	3	5

Use the table to answer the questions.

a What is the most popular food?

b What is the least popular food?

c How many children are at the picnic?

Add.
4 + 5 + 7 + 3 + 5 = 24

d How many more children brought oranges than sandwiches to the picnic?

Subtract.
7 − 4 = 3

Home Maths

In **2**, there are five children who brought apples. Explain to your child that instead of marking five I I I I I, we use the fifth tally to cross the other four tallies like this TₕₗL. This way of showing groups of five tallies makes it easy to total the tallies at the end.

3 The graph shows the number of toys that a toy shop sold in one day.

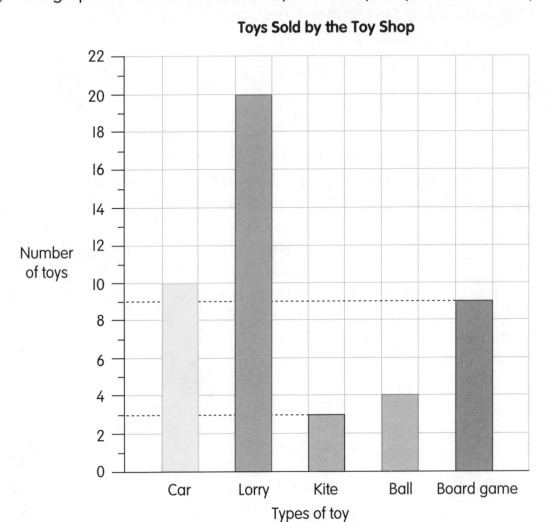

Using data from the graph, complete the following table.

Types of Toy	Number of Toys
Car	
Lorry	
Kite	
Ball	
Board game	

Look at the table on the previous page and answer the following questions.

a Which toy was the most popular?

b Which toy was the least popular?

c How many toys did the shop sell altogether?

d How many more board games than kites did the shop sell?

e The shop sold half as many ⬚ as lorries.

f The toy shop owner wants to sell twice as many kites as cars. How many more kites does he need to sell?

Activity

4 Work in a groups of four. Copy the table below. Find out how everyone in your class gets to school. Use tallies to record the data. Then count the tallies and complete the last column of the table.

How Children Come to School	Tally	Number of Children
Walk		
Bus		
Car		
Taxi		
Bicycle		

Study the table and write five questions about it. Here are some words and phrases that you could use:

how many children   fewer than   more than

the least   the most   altogether

Practice Book 4A, p.59

Let's Learn!

More tables

1 Ella draws a table to show the birthdays of a group of children in her school in the months from January to June of one year. Copy and complete the table below.

Months of Birthdays	Number of Boys	Number of Girls	Total Number
January	2	3	5
February	4		6
March		2	3
April	5		5
May	4	2	
June		3	7
Total			

Read the table and answer the following questions.

a How many children are born in May and June?

b How many children are born from January to June?

c In which month does the greatest number of children celebrate their birthdays?

d If Ella is the youngest among those born in March,
  i how many of the children born from January to June are older than her?
  ii how many of the children born from January to June are younger than her?

2 This table shows the number of 10p coins and 20p coins five children have saved in their money boxes.

| Child | 10p Coins | | 20p Coins | | Total Amount (£) |
	Number of Coins Saved	Amount Saved (£)	Number of Coins Saved	Amount Saved (£)	
Omar	12	1·20	18	3·60	4·80
Ruby	15		16		
Peter	20		10		
Millie	13		12		
Miya	6		25		
Total					

Work out the total amount that Omar has saved.

Omar has saved a total of £ [   ] .

Complete the table to find out how much the five children have saved.

a Who has saved the most coins?

b Who has saved the most money?

c How much more has Miya saved than Ruby?

d How much less has Peter saved than Ruby?

e How much more must Omar save to match the amount Miya has saved?

Activity

3 Talk to each of your friends and find out their favourite colour. Record your findings. Make a table of the data.

4   The table shows the number of drinks and sandwiches sold at four stalls during a school fair.

Stall	Drink (30p each)		Sandwich (80p each)		Total Amount (£)
	Number of Drinks Sold	Amount Collected (£)	Number of Sandwiches Sold	Amount Collected (£)	
A	25	7·50	20	16·00	23·50
B	25		10		
C	12		5		
D	30		15		
Total					

Stall A collected £23·50 by selling 25 drinks and 20 sandwiches.

Copy and complete the table to find out how much the other stalls have collected.

a   Which stall collected the most money?

b   Which stall collected the least money?

c   Which stall sold the most drinks and sandwiches?

d   Which stall sold the least drinks and sandwiches?
Give a possible reason why this stall sold the least drinks and sandwiches.

Practice Book 4A, p.63

Let's Learn!

Line graphs

1 The table shows the temperature of a room overnight.

Time	10:00p.m.	11:00p.m.	12:00p.m.	1:00a.m.	2:00a.m.	3:00a.m.
Temperature (°C)	15	8	5	7	10	12

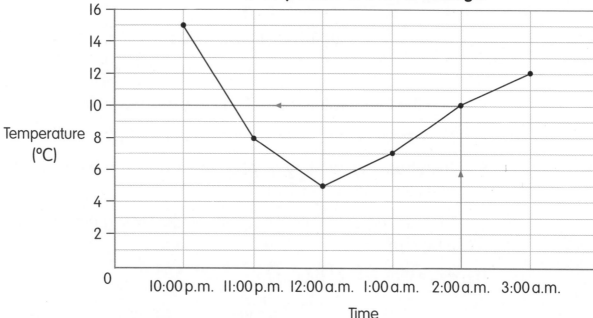

a What is the temperature at 2:00 a.m?

1 Find 2:00 a.m along the axis (green line).

2 Next move up (red arrow) until you meet the line of the graph.

3 Then from the meeting point on the graph, move left until you meet the axis (brown line).

4 The reading at the meeting point on the axis (brown line) is 10°C.

The red lines show steps 1 to 4. This is how you read temperature at different times.

The temperature at 2:00 a.m is 10°C.

b At what time was the room 8 °C?

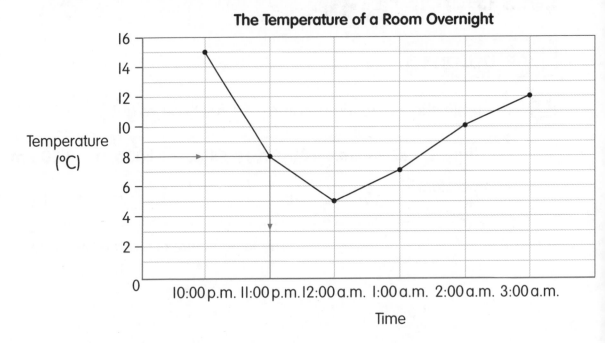

The Temperature of a Room Overnight

1 Find the temperature of 8 °C on the axis (brown line).

2 Next move right (blue arrow) until you meet the line of the graph.

3 Then from the meeting point on the graph, move down until you meet the axis (green line).

4 The reading at the meeting point on the axis (green line) is 11:00 p.m.

The room was 8 °C at 11:00 p.m.

The blue lines show steps 1 to 4. This is how you find out at which time the room was at a given temperature.

Home Maths

Encourage your child to look out for graphs in newspapers, magazines and books. Discuss the information in each graph.

2 The line graph shows the amount of petrol left in a car and the distance the car travelled. Look at the graph and answer the questions below.

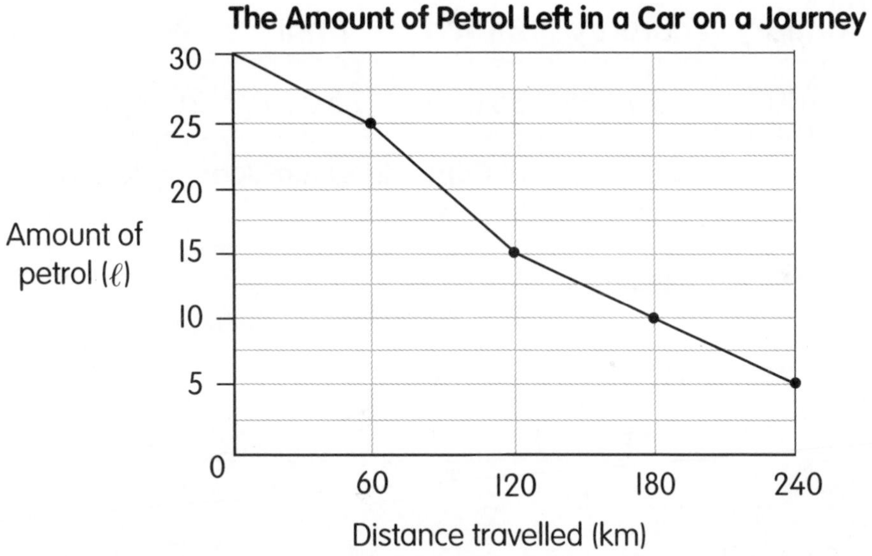

The Amount of Petrol Left in a Car on a Journey

Amount of petrol (ℓ)

Distance travelled (km)

a How much petrol was in the car at:

   i the start of the journey?

   ii the end of the journey?

b How much petrol was used for:

   i the first 60 km travelled?   **ii** the second 60 km travelled?

   iii the third 60 km travelled?   **iv** the fourth 60 km travelled?

c Look at the answers you got in **b**.

   What can you say about the amounts of petrol used?

3 The table shows the monthly sales of computers in a shop from January to June.

Month	January	February	March	April	May	June
Sales (£)	45 000	50 000	35 000	25 000	20 000	30 000

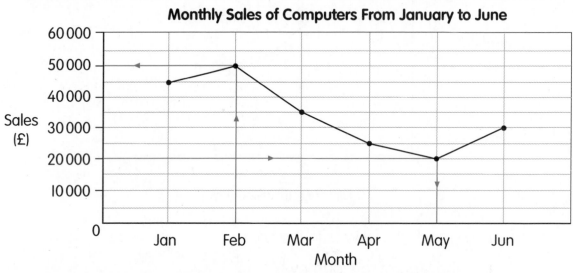

Monthly Sales of Computers From January to June

a From the graph, we can read that in February, £50 000 worth of computers were sold.

b From the graph, we can read that the shop sold £20 000 worth of computers in May.

c i £50 000 worth of computers were sold in February.
£45 000 worth of computers were sold in January.
By how much did the sales increase between these two months?

£50 000 − £45 000 = £5000

The sales increased by £5000.

ii £25 000 worth of computers were sold in April.

£ ☐ worth of computers were sold in May.

By how much did the sales decrease between these two months?

£25 000 − £ ☐ = £ ☐

The sales decreased by £ ☐ .

iii Between which other months was there an increase in the sales of computers?

d What were the sales in **i** January? **ii** June?

i £ ⬚ worth of computers were sold in January.

ii £ ⬚ worth of computers were sold in June.

e In which months were **i** £35 000 **ii** £25 000 worth of computers sold?

i In ⬚ , £35 000 worth of computers were sold.

ii In ⬚ , £25 000 worth of computers were sold.

f **i** Between which two months did sales decrease the most?

Sales decreased the most between ⬚ and ⬚ .

ii By how much did the sales decrease?

The sales decreased by £ ⬚ .

g **i** In which month were the sales twice those in April?

In ⬚ , the sales were twice those in April.

ii What was the difference in the sales between these two months?

The difference was £ ⬚ .

🏠 **Home Maths** Look at the different types of graphs featured in magazines and newspapers with your child. Encourage them to interpret the graphs.

4 The line graph shows the cost of a type of wire sold in a DIY shop.

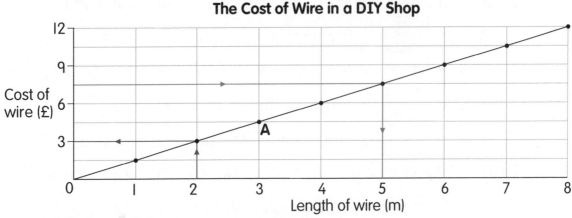

The Cost of Wire in a DIY Shop

a We can read from the graph that 2 m of wire cost £3.

b We can also read from the graph that when the cost is £7·50, the length of wire is 5 m.

> The graph is a straight line.

c Find the cost of **i** 4 m **ii** 8 m of wire.

i 4 m of wire costs £ ☐ .

ii 8 m of wire costs £ ☐ .

d Find the length of wire that costs **i** £9 **ii** £10·50.

i If the wire costs £9, the length is ☐ m.

ii If the wire costs £10·50, the length is ☐ m.

e Find the length and cost of a wire at point A on the graph.

At point A, the length of wire is ☐ m.

The cost of wire at point A is £ ☐ .

f Use the graph to find the missing numbers. What is the increase in the cost of the wire for every 1 m increase in length?

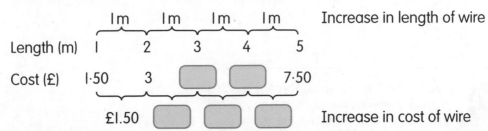

	1 m	1 m	1 m	1 m	Increase in length of wire
Length (m)	1	2	3	4	5
Cost (£)	1·50	3	☐	☐	7·50

£1.50 ☐ ☐ ☐ Increase in cost of wire

For every 1 m increase in length, the cost of the wire increases by £ ☐ .

5 Matt hung different masses on a spring and recorded his results in the line graph below. Use the graph to answer the following questions.

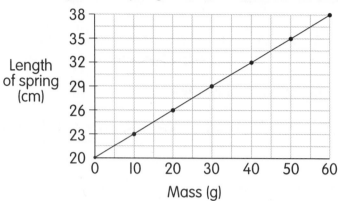

The Length of a Spring with Different Masses Attached

a What is the length of the spring when it is not stretched?

b What is the length of the spring when these masses are hung on it?

  i 10 g   **ii** 30 g   **iii** 40 g   **iv** 50 g

c What is the mass hung on the spring when its length is:

  i 26 cm?   **ii** 38 cm?

d By how many centimetres is the spring stretched when a mass of 60 g is hung on it?

e If the spring is stretched by 15 cm, what is the mass that is hung on it?

Maths Journal

6 Write down which parts of the unit you like the most and which parts you find difficult.

Presenting and interpreting data in a table:
  a Use data from tallies to complete a table.
  b Use data from a bar graph to complete a table.
  c Solve problems using data presented in tables.

Line graphs:
  a Obtain information by reading the scales on line graphs.
  b Solve problems using information presented in line graphs.

Practice Book 4A, p.65

Put On Your Thinking Caps!

7 The tables below show the number of letters delivered by Mr Evans and Mrs Simpson from Monday to Thursday last week.

Letters Delivered by Mr Evans

Day	Monday	Tuesday	Wednesday	Thursday
Number of Letters Delivered	125	150	180	240

Letters Delivered by Mrs Simpson

Day	Monday	Tuesday	Wednesday	Thursday
Number of Letters Delivered	160	235	110	185

Look at the tables and answer the following questions.

a How many letters did Mr Evans and Mrs Simpson deliver altogether on Tuesday?

b How many letters did Mr Evans and Mrs Simpson deliver altogether from Monday to Thursday?

c On which days did Mr Evans deliver more letters than Mrs Simpson?

d On which days did Mr Evans deliver more than 150 letters?

e On which days did Mrs Simpson deliver more than 180 letters?

f How many more letters would Mr Evans have to deliver on Tuesday in order to match the number of letters delivered by Mrs Simpson on the same day?

Practice Book 4A, p.69

Unit
5 Fractions

Let's Learn!

Mixed numbers

  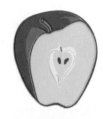

| I whole | I whole | I half |

$$2 + \frac{1}{2} = 2\frac{1}{2}$$

There are $2\frac{1}{2}$ apples.

$2\frac{1}{2}$ is a mixed number.

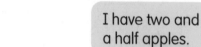
I have two and a half apples.

When you add a whole number and a fraction, you get a **mixed number**.

2 Jack drinks 3 bottles of water. Millie drinks $\frac{1}{4}$ bottle of water.

How much water do they drink altogether?

$3 + \frac{1}{4} = \boxed{}$

They drink $\boxed{}$ bottles of water altogether.

What mixed number does each of the following represent?

a

I whole

3 quarters

$$1 + \frac{3}{4} =$$

b

I whole

I whole

3 eighths

$$2 + \frac{3}{8} =$$

c

I whole

I whole

5 sixths

$$2 + \frac{5}{6} =$$

d

I whole

2 thirds

$$1 + \frac{2}{3} =$$

e

I whole

I whole

3 quarters

$$2 + \frac{3}{4} =$$

Activity

4 Work in pairs.

a You will need some fraction discs. Take turns to show the mixed numbers below using the fraction discs.

$1\frac{1}{2}$ $2\frac{3}{4}$ $3\frac{3}{4}$ $4\frac{1}{2}$ $5\frac{1}{4}$ $2\frac{3}{5}$ $3\frac{5}{8}$ $4\frac{5}{6}$

b Draw pictures to show the mixed numbers below.

$1\frac{1}{4}$ $2\frac{1}{2}$ $3\frac{3}{4}$ $4\frac{1}{2}$ $2\frac{3}{4}$ $3\frac{1}{2}$ $5\frac{1}{4}$ $4\frac{1}{4}$ $5\frac{1}{2}$

5 Fill in the boxes to show the wholes and parts shaded. Then write the mixed number.

a

☐ wholes ☐ parts = ☐

b

☐ wholes ☐ parts = ☐

6 What number does each letter represent?

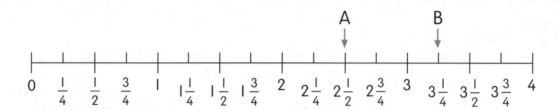

A shows $2\frac{1}{2}$ on the number line.

B shows [ ] on the number line.

You can show mixed numbers on a number line.

7 Where are $1\frac{4}{5}$ and $2\frac{1}{5}$ on the number line?

8 Copy the number line and mark the following mixed numbers.

$$1\frac{1}{2}, \ 2\frac{1}{2}, \ 3\frac{1}{2}$$

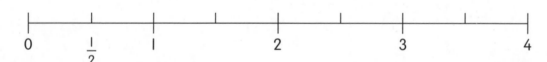

9 Simplify the fraction shown by the shaded parts.

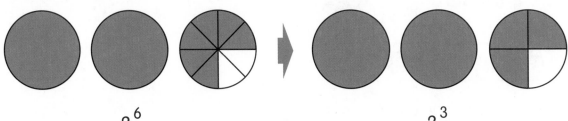

$$2\frac{6}{8}$$

$$=$$

$$2\frac{3}{4}$$

$$2\frac{6^3}{8^4} = 2\frac{3}{4}$$

Cancellation is another way of dividing both the numerator and denominator by the same number.

10 Express each mixed number in its simplest form.

a $3\frac{8}{10} = 3\frac{\Box}{\Box}$

b $1\frac{9}{12} = 1\frac{\Box}{\Box}$

c $1\frac{4}{6} = 1\frac{\Box}{\Box}$

d $4\frac{6}{9} = 4\frac{\Box}{\Box}$

11 What are the missing numerator and denominator?

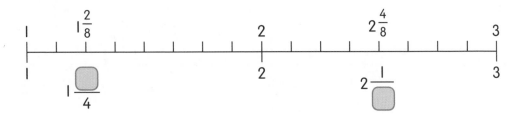

Practice Book 4A, p.79

Let's Learn!

Improper fractions

1 Ruby has some pieces of ribbon.

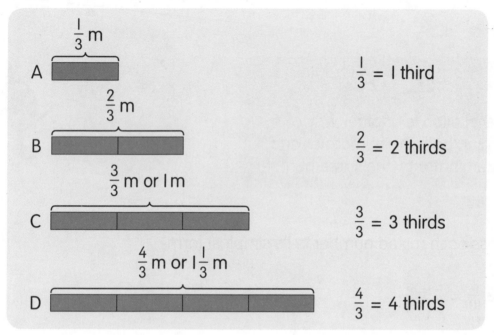

Look at piece D. It is $1\frac{1}{3}$ m long.

There are 4 thirds in $1\frac{1}{3}$.

$1\frac{1}{3} = \frac{1}{3} + \frac{1}{3} + \frac{1}{3} + \frac{1}{3}$

$\quad = \frac{4}{3}$

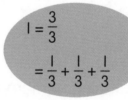

$1 = \frac{3}{3}$

$\quad = \frac{1}{3} + \frac{1}{3} + \frac{1}{3}$

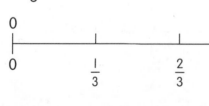

improper fractions

$\frac{3}{3}, \frac{4}{3}, \frac{5}{3}$ and $\frac{6}{3}$ are equal to or greater than 1.
They are called **improper fractions**.

2 Write an improper fraction for the shaded parts.

 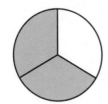

There are 5 thirds in $1\frac{2}{3}$.

$1\frac{2}{3} = \frac{1}{3} + \frac{1}{3} + \frac{1}{3} + \frac{1}{3} + \frac{1}{3}$

$\quad = \frac{5}{3}$

3 Write an improper fraction for the shaded parts.

a

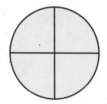 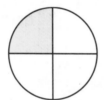

There are ☐ quarters in $1\frac{1}{4}$.

$1\frac{1}{4} = ☐ + ☐ + ☐ + ☐ + ☐$

$\quad = ☐$

b

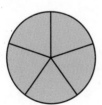 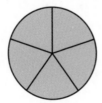 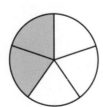

There are ☐ fifths in $2\frac{2}{5}$.

$2\frac{2}{5} = ☐$

4 How many halves are there in $2\frac{1}{2}$?

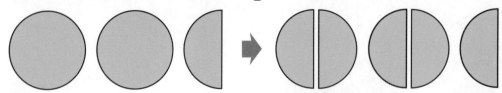

There are 5 halves in $2\frac{1}{2}$.

5 halves = $\frac{5}{2}$

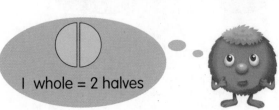

1 whole = 2 halves

5 Express each of the following as an improper fraction.

a

There are ⬜ quarters in $1\frac{3}{4}$.

⬜ quarters = ⬜

1 whole = 4 quarters

b

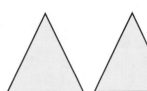

There are ⬜ halves in 3.

⬜ halves = ⬜

c

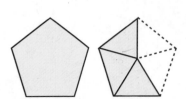

There are ⬜ fifths in $1\frac{3}{5}$.

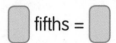

⬜ fifths = ⬜

Activity

6 Work in pairs.
Draw pictures to show the improper fractions below.

 $\frac{5}{3}$ $\frac{5}{4}$ $\frac{8}{5}$ $\frac{7}{7}$

Example

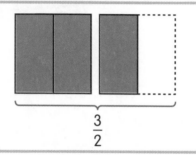

$\frac{3}{2}$

Here is a picture to show the improper fraction $\frac{3}{2}$.

7 Simplify the fraction shown by the shaded parts.

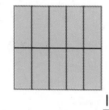 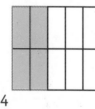   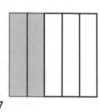

$\frac{14}{10}$ $\frac{7}{5}$

$\frac{14^7}{10_5} = \frac{7}{5}$

8 Express each improper fraction in its simplest form.

a $\frac{15}{6} = \dfrac{\Box}{\Box}$

b $\frac{26}{12} = \dfrac{\Box}{\Box}$

9 What are the missing improper fractions?

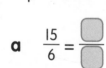

0   1 $1\frac{1}{6}$ $1\frac{1}{3}$ $1\frac{2}{3}$ $1\frac{5}{6}$ 2

0          $\frac{1}{3}$ $\frac{2}{3}$ $\frac{5}{6}$ $\frac{3}{3}$ $\frac{7}{6}$ $\frac{4}{3}$ $\Box$ $\Box$ $\Box$

Practice Book 4A, p.85

95

Let's Learn!

Conversion of fractions

1 Change $\frac{4}{3}$ to a mixed number.

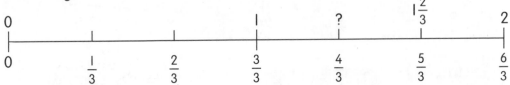

$\frac{4}{3}$ is an improper fraction.

$\frac{4}{3}$ = 4 thirds

   = 3 thirds + 1 third

   = $\frac{3}{3}$ + $\frac{1}{3}$

   = 1 + $\frac{1}{3}$

   = $1\frac{1}{3}$

2 Change $\frac{13}{5}$ to a mixed number.

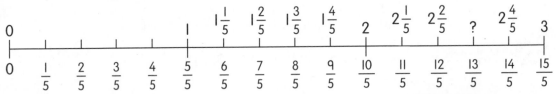

$\frac{13}{5}$ = ☐ fifths

   = ☐ fifths + ☐ fifths

   = ☐ + ☐

   = ☐ + ☐

   = ☐

$\frac{5}{5}$ = $\frac{1}{1}$ = 1 (÷ 5)

$\frac{10}{5}$ = $\frac{2}{1}$ = 2 (÷ 5)

3 Change $\frac{7}{3}$ to a mixed number.

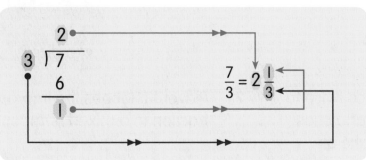

Here is another method for conversion using the division rule.

First divide the numerator by the denominator.

$$7 \div 3 = 2 \, r \, 1$$

There are 2 wholes and 1 third in $\frac{7}{3}$.

$$\frac{7}{3} = 2\frac{1}{3}$$

4 Change the improper fractions to mixed numbers using the division rule.

a $\frac{15}{4} = \boxed{}$

b $\frac{13}{6} = \boxed{}$

5 Change $\frac{15}{9}$ to a mixed number in its simplest form. Then check your answer using the division rule.

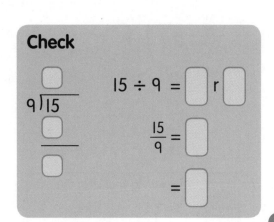

$\frac{15}{9} = \boxed{}$ ninths

$= \boxed{}$ ninths $+ \boxed{}$ ninths

$= \boxed{} + \boxed{}$

$= \boxed{} + \boxed{}$

$= \boxed{} = \boxed{}$

Check

$$9 \overline{)15}$$

$$15 \div 9 = \boxed{} \, r \, \boxed{}$$

$$\frac{15}{9} = \boxed{}$$

$$= \boxed{}$$

Activity

6 How to play:

Players: 4
You will need:
• a dice

1 Player 1 rolls the dice twice to get two numbers, and uses the numbers to make an improper fraction.

2 Player 1 changes the improper fraction to a mixed number.

3 The other players check the answer. Player 1 gets a point if the answer is correct.

Take turns to play. Play at least 4 rounds. The player with the highest score wins!

7 Change $3\frac{3}{4}$ to an improper fraction.

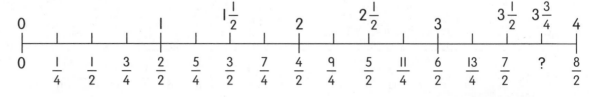

$3\frac{3}{4} = 3 + \frac{3}{4}$

$= \frac{12}{4} + \frac{3}{4}$

$= \frac{15}{4}$

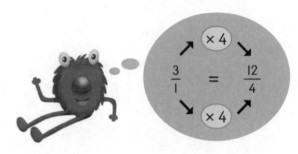

Explain to your child that:

$3 = 3 \div 1$
$= \frac{3}{1}$

$1\overline{)3}$

Home Maths

8 Change $4\frac{1}{3}$ to an improper fraction.

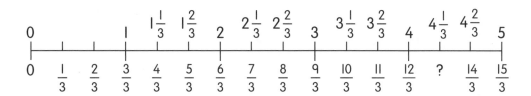

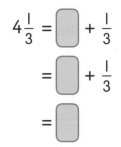

$$4\frac{1}{3} = \boxed{} + \frac{1}{3}$$

$$= \boxed{} + \frac{1}{3}$$

$$= \boxed{}$$

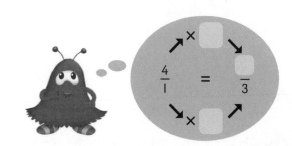

9 Change the mixed number to an improper fraction.

$$5\frac{2}{3} = \boxed{} + \frac{2}{3}$$

$$= \frac{\boxed{}}{3} + \frac{2}{3}$$

$$= \frac{\boxed{}}{3}$$

10 Change $3\frac{1}{2}$ to an improper fraction.

First multiply the whole number by the denominator.
$3 \times 2 = 6$

Next add the result to the numerator 1.
$6 + 1 = 7$

There are 7 halves in $3\frac{1}{2}$.

$$3\frac{1}{2} = \frac{7}{2}$$

Here is another method for conversion using the multiplication rule.

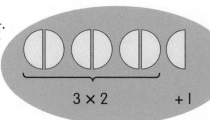

3×2 $+ 1$

11 Use the multiplication rule to change the mixed numbers to improper fractions.

a $3\frac{1}{5}$

b $4\frac{6}{9}$

12 Change the mixed numbers to improper fractions.

a $1\frac{6}{5} = \boxed{}$

b $3\frac{2}{5} = \boxed{}$

13 Change the mixed number to an improper fraction in its simplest form.

$6\frac{6}{8} = \boxed{} + \frac{6}{8}$

$\quad = \boxed{} + \frac{6}{8}$

$\quad = \boxed{}$

$\quad = \boxed{}$

Check

$6\frac{6}{8}$

$6 \times \boxed{} = \boxed{}$

$\boxed{} + 6 = \boxed{}$

There are $\boxed{}$ eighths in $6\frac{6}{8}$.

There are $\boxed{}$ quarters in $6\frac{6}{8}$.

Practice Book 4A, p.89

Let's Learn!

Adding and subtracting fractions

1 Anna and Sarah have an apple each. Anna eats $\frac{7}{8}$ of her apple and Sarah eats $\frac{3}{4}$ of her apple. What fraction of apples do they eat altogether?

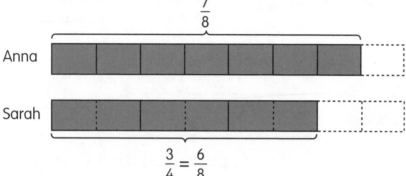

$$\frac{7}{8} + \frac{3}{4} = \frac{7}{8} + \frac{6}{8}$$

$$= \frac{13}{8}$$

$$= \frac{8}{8} + \frac{5}{8}$$

$$= 1 + \frac{5}{8}$$

$$= 1\frac{5}{8}$$

They eat $1\frac{5}{8}$ apples altogether.

2 Find the sum of $\frac{3}{4}$, $\frac{1}{8}$ and $\frac{5}{8}$.

$$\frac{3}{4} + \frac{1}{8} + \frac{5}{8} = \frac{6}{8} + \frac{1}{8} + \frac{5}{8}$$

$$= \frac{12}{8}$$

$$= \frac{3}{2}$$

$$= 1\frac{1}{2}$$

The sum of $\frac{3}{4}$, $\frac{1}{8}$ and $\frac{5}{8}$ is $1\frac{1}{2}$.

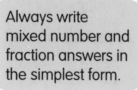

Always write mixed number and fraction answers in the simplest form.

3 Add and express the answer in its simplest form.

Please don't include any improper fractions in your answers.

a $\frac{7}{9} + \frac{2}{3}$

b $\frac{5}{6} + \frac{1}{12} + \frac{2}{12}$

c $\frac{1}{3} + \frac{5}{12}$

d $\frac{3}{4} + \frac{3}{8}$

4 Mario has 3 swiss rolls. He eats $\frac{4}{9}$ of one swiss roll. What fraction of the swiss rolls is left?

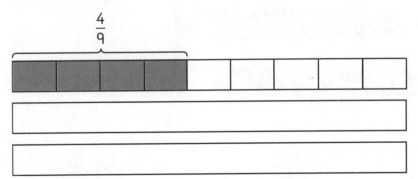

Method 1

$$3 - \frac{4}{9} = 2\frac{9}{9} - \frac{4}{9}$$
$$= 2\frac{5}{9}$$

$3 = 2 + 1$
$= 2 + \frac{9}{9}$
$= 2\frac{9}{9}$

Method 2

$$3 - \frac{4}{9} = \frac{27}{9} - \frac{4}{9}$$
$$= \frac{23}{9}$$
$$= 2\frac{5}{9}$$

$$\begin{array}{r} 2 \\ 9\overline{)23} \\ \underline{18} \\ 5 \end{array}$$

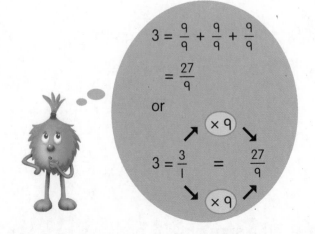

$3 = \frac{9}{9} + \frac{9}{9} + \frac{9}{9}$
$= \frac{27}{9}$

or

$3 = \frac{3}{1} \quad \xrightarrow{\times 9} \quad = \quad \frac{27}{9} \quad \xleftarrow{\times 9}$

$2\frac{5}{9}$ of the swiss rolls are left.

5 Find the difference between 2 and $\frac{3}{8}$.

Method 1

$$2 - \frac{3}{8} = 1\frac{8}{8} - \frac{3}{8}$$

$$= 1\frac{5}{8}$$

$$2 = 1 + 1$$
$$= 1 + \frac{8}{8}$$
$$= 1\frac{8}{8}$$

Method 2

$$2 - \frac{3}{8} = \frac{16}{8} - \frac{3}{8}$$

$$= \frac{13}{8}$$

$$= 1\frac{5}{8}$$

$$2 = \frac{8}{8} + \frac{8}{8}$$
$$= \frac{16}{8}$$
or
$$2 = \frac{2}{1} \overset{\times 8}{=} \frac{16}{8} \quad (\times 8)$$

6 Find the difference between $\frac{5}{6}$ and $\frac{7}{12}$.

$$\frac{5}{6} \overset{\times 2}{=} \frac{\square}{12} \quad (\times 2)$$

$$\frac{\square}{12} - \frac{7}{12} = \frac{\square}{12}$$

$$= \frac{\square}{\square}$$

7 Subtract. Express each answer in its simplest form.

a $2 - \frac{5}{12}$

b $5 - \frac{2}{9}$

c $\frac{3}{4} - \frac{5}{12}$

d $\frac{8}{9} - \frac{1}{3}$

Practice Book 4A, p.93

Let's Learn!

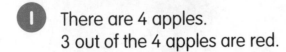

1 There are 4 apples.
3 out of the 4 apples are red.

How many of the apples are red? Give your answer as a fraction.

$\frac{3}{4}$ of the apples are red.

Here is a set of 12 apples.
The set of apples is divided into 4 equal groups.
3 out of the 4 groups of apples are red.

$\frac{3}{4}$ is 3 out of 4 equal groups.

How many of the apples are red? Give your answer as a fraction.

$\frac{3}{4}$ of the apples are red.

Home Maths

Encourage your child to talk about fractions of a set.
For example, if you have bought 3 oranges and 5
apples, ask "What fraction of the fruit is oranges?"

2

a   How many of the ducks are yellow? Give your answer as a fraction.

☐ of the ducks are yellow.

b   How many of the ducks are pink? Give your answer as a fraction.

☐ of the ducks are pink.

3

There are 16 cups in the set. 12 out of the 16 cups in the set are blue.
$\frac{3}{4}$ of the cups are blue. $\frac{3}{4}$ of 16 is 12.

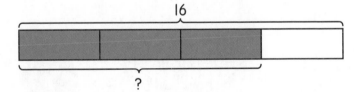

The shaded parts make up $\frac{3}{4}$ of the set.

What is $\frac{3}{4}$ of 16?

4 units = 16
1 unit = 16 ÷ 4 = 4
3 units = 4 × 3 = 12

So $\frac{3}{4}$ of 16 is 12.

You can show fractions
of a set using a model.

4 Find the value of $\frac{2}{5}$ of 15.

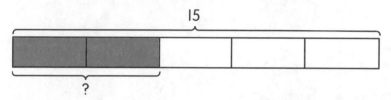

5 units = ☐

I unit = ☐

2 units = ☐

So $\frac{2}{5}$ of 15 is ☐.

Divide 15 into 5 equal parts.
The shaded parts = $\frac{2}{5}$ of the set.

Activity

5 Work in pairs. Draw models to find the value of the following:

Example

$\frac{2}{3}$ of 6

3 units = 6

I unit = 6 ÷ 3 = 2

2 units = 2 × 2 = 4

So $\frac{2}{3}$ of 6 is 4.

Here is a model
to show $\frac{2}{3}$ of 6.

a $\frac{2}{3}$ of 9

b $\frac{3}{5}$ of 30

6 Here is a shorter method to find $\frac{3}{4}$ of 16.

Make sure you cancel common factors!

Method I

$\frac{3}{4}$ of $16 = \frac{3}{\overset{}{\underset{1}{4}}} \times \overset{4}{16}$

$= 3 \times 4$

$= 12$

Method 2

$\frac{3}{4} \times 16 = \frac{3 \times 16}{4}$

$= \frac{48}{4}$

$= 12$

The product of $\frac{3}{4}$ and 16 can be written as

$\frac{3}{4} \times 16$ or $16 \times \frac{3}{4}$.

7 Use the methods in **6** to find the values of the following:

a $\frac{1}{3}$ of 12

b $\frac{3}{4}$ of 20

c $\frac{4}{5}$ of 25

d $\frac{5}{7}$ of 28

8 The model shows a set of objects. What fraction of the set does the shaded part show?

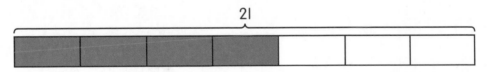

21

The shaded part shows $\frac{\square}{\square}$ of $\boxed{}$.

Home Maths

Explain to your child that $\frac{3}{4}$ **of** 16 is equivalent to $\frac{3}{4} \times 16$. Help them to find fractions of a set using money. For example, spend $\frac{2}{5}$ of £2 = 80p; save $\frac{1}{4}$ of £2 = 50p etc.

Practice Book 4A, p.95

Let's Learn!

Word problems

1 Mr Jones needs some flour to bake bread. He borrows $\frac{1}{4}$ kg of flour from Mr Lee and $\frac{7}{8}$ kg of flour from Miss Green.

How much flour does he borrow altogether?

$$\frac{1}{4} + \frac{7}{8} = \frac{2}{8} + \frac{7}{8}$$

$$= \frac{9}{8}$$

$$= 1\frac{1}{8}$$

He borrows $1\frac{1}{8}$ kg of flour altogether.

2 Ravi, Hannah and Tom each drink different amounts of water.
Ravi drinks $\frac{5}{6}$ ℓ of water. Hannah drinks $\frac{7}{12}$ ℓ of water and Tom drinks $\frac{11}{12}$ ℓ of water.

How much water do they drink altogether?

$$\frac{5}{6} + \frac{7}{12} + \frac{11}{12} = \boxed{} + \frac{7}{12} + \frac{11}{12}$$

$$= \boxed{}$$

$$= \boxed{}$$

$$= \boxed{}$$

They drink $\boxed{}$ ℓ of water altogether.

3 Mrs Thompson has 9 m of ribbon. She sells $\frac{1}{5}$ m in the morning and $\frac{7}{10}$ m in the afternoon.
How much ribbon does she have left?

Method 1

$$9 - \frac{1}{5} - \frac{7}{10} = 8\frac{10}{10} - \frac{1}{5} - \frac{7}{10}$$
$$= 8\frac{10}{10} - \frac{2}{10} - \frac{7}{10}$$
$$= 8\frac{1}{10}$$

Method 2

$$\frac{1}{5} + \frac{7}{10} = \frac{2}{10} + \frac{7}{10}$$
$$= \frac{9}{10}$$
$$9 - \frac{9}{10} = 8\frac{10}{10} - \frac{9}{10}$$
$$= 8\frac{1}{10}$$

She has $8\frac{1}{10}$ m of ribbon left.

4 Emma has to travel 12 km from Smithstown to Philipstown. She travels $\frac{5}{8}$ km by bicycle. Then she travels another $\frac{1}{4}$ km by car until the car breaks down.

How far is she from Philipstown when the car breaks down?

Method 1

$$12 - \frac{5}{8} - \frac{1}{4} = 11\frac{\boxed{}}{\boxed{}} - \frac{5}{8} - \frac{1}{4}$$
$$= \boxed{} - \frac{5}{8} - \frac{\boxed{}}{\boxed{}}$$
$$= \boxed{}$$

Method 2

$$\boxed{} + \boxed{} = \boxed{} + \boxed{}$$
$$= \boxed{}$$
$$\boxed{} - \boxed{} = \boxed{} - \boxed{}$$
$$= \boxed{}$$

She is $\boxed{}$ km from Philipstown.

5 Mrs Brown has 9 roses.
6 of them are red. The rest are yellow.

 a What fraction of the roses is red?

 b What fraction of the roses is yellow?

 a 6 out of 9 is $\frac{6}{9}$.

$$\frac{6^{2}}{9^{3}} = \frac{2}{3}$$

$\frac{2}{3}$ of the roses are red.

3 is a common factor of 6 and 9.
Divide 6 and 9 by 3:
$6 \div 3 = 2$
$9 \div 3 = 3$

You get $\frac{2}{3}$.

 b $1 - \frac{2}{3} = \frac{3}{3} - \frac{2}{3}$

$$= \frac{1}{3}$$

$\frac{1}{3}$ of the roses are yellow.

6 Matt has a piece of string 1 m long.
He cuts off 18 cm of it.

 a What fraction of the string does he cut off?

 b What fraction of the string is left?

 a 18 out of 100 is $\frac{18}{100}$.

$$\frac{18}{100} = \boxed{}$$

$\boxed{}$ of the string is cut off.

Change 1 m
to 100 cm.

 b $1 - \boxed{} = \boxed{}$

$\boxed{}$ of the string is left.

7 Millie buys some flowers. $\frac{2}{5}$ of them are roses.
She buys 12 roses.

How many flowers does Millie buy altogether?

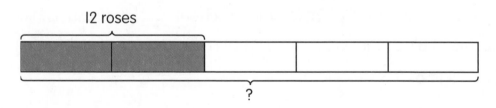

12 roses

?

2 units = 12
1 unit = 12 ÷ 2
        = 6

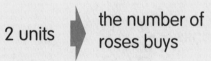

2 units → the number of roses buys

5 units = 6 × 5
        = 30

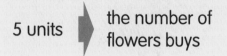

5 units → the number of flowers buys

Millie buys 30 flowers altogether.

8 Peter's dad spent $\frac{4}{7}$ of his money on a pair of shoes.

The shoes cost £48. How much money did he have at first?

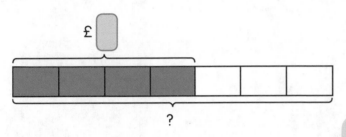

£ ⬜

?

4 units = £ ⬜

I unit = £ ⬜ ◯ ⬜ = £ ⬜

7 units = £ ⬜ ◯ ⬜ = £ ⬜

He had £ ⬜ at first.

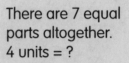
There are 7 equal parts altogether.
4 units = ?

9 A painter is mixing green paint to paint a school. $\frac{2}{5}$ of the paint is blue.
The volume of blue paint is 25 litres. What is the volume of yellow paint?

2 units = 25 litres

I unit = $\frac{25}{2}$

3 units = $\frac{25}{2} \times 3$

  = $\frac{⬜}{⬜}$

  = ⬜ litres

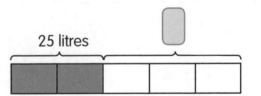

25 litres

The volume of yellow paint is ⬜ litres.

10 Isabel has 18 stickers. She gives away $\frac{1}{3}$ of them.

How many stickers does she have left?

Method 1

$$\frac{1}{\cancel{3}_1} \times \cancel{18}^{6} = 1 \times 6$$
$$= 6$$

She gives away 6 stickers.

$18 - 6 = 12$

She has 12 stickers left.

First find the number of stickers Isabel gives away.

Method 2

$$1 - \frac{1}{3} = \frac{3}{3} - \frac{1}{3}$$
$$= \frac{2}{3}$$

First find what fraction of the stickers she has left.

She has $\frac{2}{3}$ of the stickers left.

$$\frac{2}{\cancel{3}_1} \times \cancel{18}^{6} = 2 \times 6$$
$$= 12$$

She has 12 stickers left.

Method 3

3 units = 18
1 unit $= 18 \div 3$
$\quad\quad = 6$
She gives away 6 stickers.

2 units = 6 × 2
$\quad\quad = 12$

Isabel has 12 stickers left.

18 stickers

given away   ?

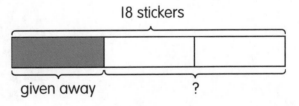

1 unit → the number of stickers Isabel gives away

2 units → the number of stickers Isabel has left

11 Daniel has £50. He uses $\frac{3}{5}$ of it to buy a coat.

How much money does he have left?

Method 1

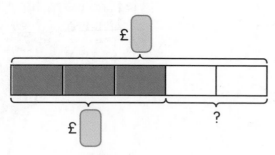

£ ☐

£ ☐   ?

£ ☐

5 units = £ ☐

1 unit = £ ☐ ◯ ☐

       = £ ☐

2 units = £ ☐ ◯ ☐

       = £ ☐

He has £ ☐ left.

Method 2

$\frac{3}{5}$ of £50 = $\frac{☐}{☐}$ × £ ☐

            = ☐ × £ ☐

            = £ ☐

Daniel spends £ ☐ on the coat.

£ ☐ – £ ☐ = £ ☐

He has £ ☐ left.

Solve these word problems.

12 Meena measures the length of three ropes. Rope A is $\frac{1}{2}$ m long. Rope B is $\frac{5}{8}$ m long and Rope C is $\frac{3}{8}$ m long. What is the total length of the three ropes?

13 Mr Thomson is mixing some paint. He mixes $\frac{3}{4}$ ℓ of red paint with $\frac{11}{12}$ ℓ of blue paint.

   a What volume of purple paint does he have?

   b If he has 8 ℓ of red paint in the beginning, what is the volume of red paint left?

14 Nick has 10 toy cars. 4 of them are red and the rest are blue.

   a What fraction of the cars is red?

   b What fraction of the cars is blue?

15 A baker bought 24 kg of flour. She used $\frac{3}{8}$ of it to make bread.

   a How much flour did she use?

   b How much flour did she have left?

16 Rosa spends a total of £36 on a dress and a pair of shoes.
The dress costs $\frac{4}{9}$ of the total amount spent.
How much money does Rosa spend on the shoes?

17 Mr Green makes some sandwiches for a party.

$\frac{1}{4}$ of them are cheese sandwiches.

The rest are chicken sandwiches.
He makes 32 cheese sandwiches.
How many sandwiches does he make altogether?

Maths Journal

18 Write down which parts of the unit you like the most and which parts you find difficult.

    a   Mixed numbers

    b   Improper fractions

    c   Conversion of fractions

    d   Adding and subtracting fractions

    e   Fractions of a set

    f   Word problems

Write three or four sentences on how fractions can help you in your daily life.

Practice Book 4A, p.99

Put On Your Thinking Caps!

19 Ava has a whole chocolate bar.
Ethan has only part of an identical chocolate bar.

Ava gives $\frac{1}{4}$ of her chocolate bar to Ethan.

In the end, both children have the same amount of chocolate.

What fraction of a chocolate bar did Ethan have at first?

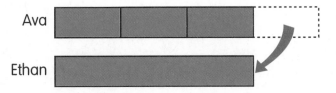

Here are 2 equal bars to show that both children had an equal amount of chocolate in the end.

Work backwards to find the fraction of the chocolate bar Ethan had at first.

Practice Book 4A, p.106   Practice Book 4A, p.108

Unit 6 — Angles

Let's Learn!

Understanding angles

Naming angles

1

An angle is made by two lines meeting at a point.

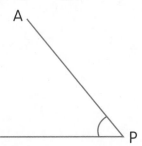

AP and BP are lines meeting at **P**.
The point P is called the **vertex**.

We can name the angle at the vertex P either ∠APB or ∠BPA.

If we label the angle at vertex P as x, we can also name it ∠x.

2 Name the angles.

Angle at P = ∠ ⬜

Angle at Q = ∠ ⬜

Angle at R = ∠ ⬜

Angle at S = ∠ ⬜

3 Name the angles labelled at the vertices A, B, C and D in another way.

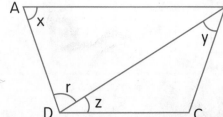

∠x = ∠ ⬜

∠y = ∠ ⬜

∠z = ∠ ⬜

∠r = ∠ ⬜

Measuring angles

We measure angles in degrees.
90 degrees is written as 90°.

We use a protractor to measure an angle in degrees.

Here is how we use a protractor to measure an angle.

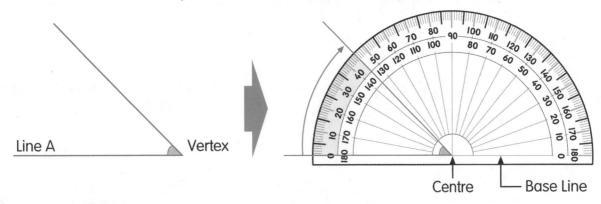

Line A   Vertex

Centre   Base Line

I   Place the base line of the protractor on Line A.

2   Place the centre of the base line of the protractor at the vertex of the angle.

3   Read the outer scale. The line passes through the 45° mark. The angle is 45°.

We read the outer scale because the zero on the outer scale lies on Line A.

2 Measure angle DEF.

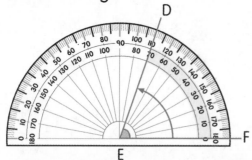

Angle DEF is smaller than a right angle. It is 70 degrees.

∠DEF = ☐

Read the inner scale, as the zero of the inner scale is on the side EF of ∠DEF.

3 Measure angle GHI.

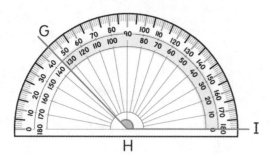

Is angle GHI smaller or greater than 90°?

Angle GHI is 135 degrees.

∠GHI = ☐

Why do we read the inner scale of the protractor?

4 Measure angle JKL.

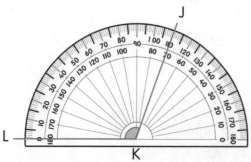

Is angle JKL smaller or greater than 90°?

Angle JKL is ☐ degrees.

∠JKL = ☐

Do we read the inner or outer scale? Why?

P6109

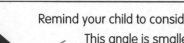

Remind your child to consider if the angle size is reasonable.

This angle is smaller than 90° so its value should be less than 90°.

This angle is greater than 90° so its value should be more than 90°.

Home Maths

5 What is the size of each angle?

a

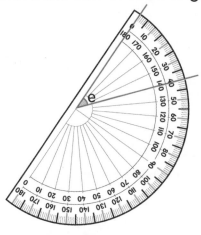

b

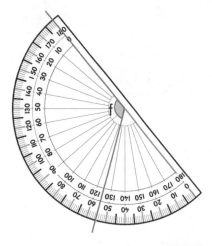

∠e = ⬚

∠f = ⬚

Activity

6 Work in pairs. Estimate and use a protractor to measure each angle.

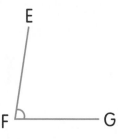

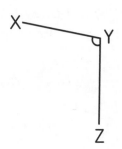

Record your answers in a table like this:

Name of Angle	Our Guess	Our Answer Using Measurement
∠ABC	80°	90°

Home Maths Encourage your child to find and measure angles on things around the home.

Practice Book 4A, p.109

Let's Learn!

Drawing angles to 180°

1 How do you draw an angle equal to 70°?

1 Draw a straight line and mark a point on the line.

2 Place the base line of the protractor on the line that you have drawn and the centre of the base line on the point.

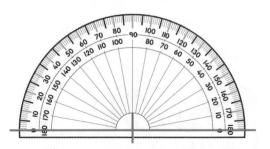

3 Use the inner scale or the outer scale to measure an angle equal to 70°. Make a mark with a dot as shown. Then draw a line through the mark to meet the point on the straight line.

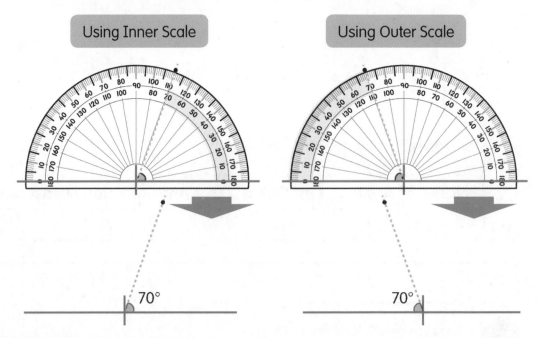

Using Inner Scale   Using Outer Scale

70°   70°

2 This is how you draw an angle equal to 145°.

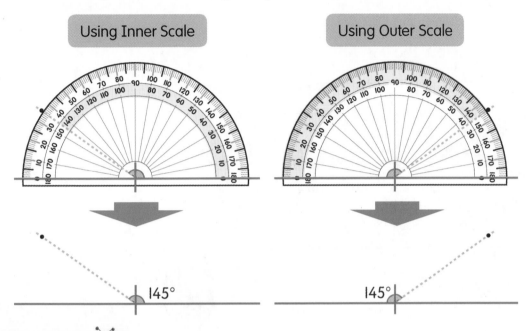

Using Inner Scale	Using Outer Scale

145°   145°

Activity

3 Work with a partner. Use a protractor to draw an angle:

a greater than 90° but smaller than 125°.

b greater than 10° but smaller than 25°.

c greater than 100° but smaller than 180°.

Example

An angle greater than 30°
but smaller than 60°

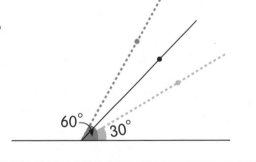

60°   30°

Help your child to draw angles that are:

Home Maths   **a** smaller than 90°.   **b** 90°.   **c** greater than 90°.

4 Draw a straight line AB. Then draw an angle at point A:

  a 45° above the line AB.

  b 45° below the line AB.

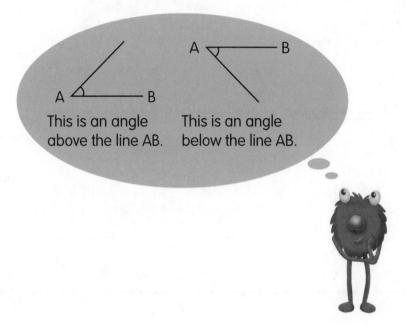

This is an angle above the line AB.

This is an angle below the line AB.

5 Draw a straight line PQ. Then draw an angle at point Q:

  a 120° above the line PQ.

  b 120° below the line PQ.

Home Maths

Check that the angles drawn are reasonable. For example, an angle of 45° should be half the size of a right angle, and an angle of 100° should be more than the size of a right angle.

Practice Book 4A, p.113

Let's Learn!

Turns and right angles

1

I right angle	2 right angles

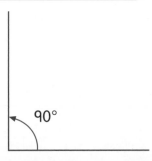

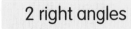

$\frac{1}{4}$ of a complete turn is 90°.

$\frac{1}{2}$ of a complete turn is 180°.

3 right angles	4 right angles

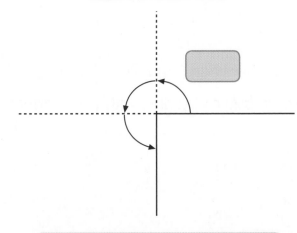

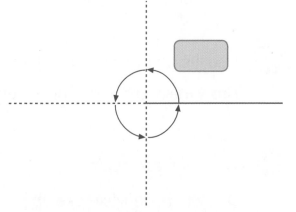

$\frac{3}{4}$ of a complete turn is 270°.

I complete turn is 360°.

2 Work in pairs to make a pair of angle strips. You will need 2 paper strips, a fastener and a sheet of paper.

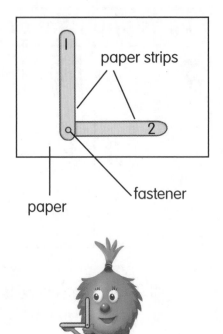

paper strips

fastener

paper

1 Stick strip 2 on the paper. Fasten strip 1 onto strip 2 so that only strip 1 moves. This is a pair of angle strips.

2 Turn strip 1 to make the following turns:

- $\frac{1}{4}$ turn,

- $\frac{1}{2}$ turn,

- $\frac{3}{4}$ turn and

- 1 complete turn.

3 Draw and label the angle made by each of the above turns.

3 Use the angle strips to make an angle between $\frac{1}{2}$ turn and $\frac{3}{4}$ turn.

Draw the angle. Make and draw more angles like this with your partner.

4 Answer these questions.

a 2 right angles make up ⬚ .

b 4 right angles is the same as ⬚ complete turn.

c What fraction of a complete turn is 270°? ⬚

Practice Book 4A, p.117

Let's Learn!

8-point compass

1 Look at the 8-point compass.

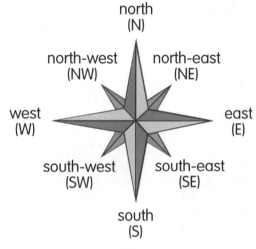

The 8-point compass shows direction.

2 The hands of a clock move in the direction shown.

So we name the direction of the following movements as:

clockwise   anti-clockwise

Movement in the same direction as the hands of a clock.   Movement in the opposite direction to the hands of a clock.

3 Ruby stands in the middle of an open field.

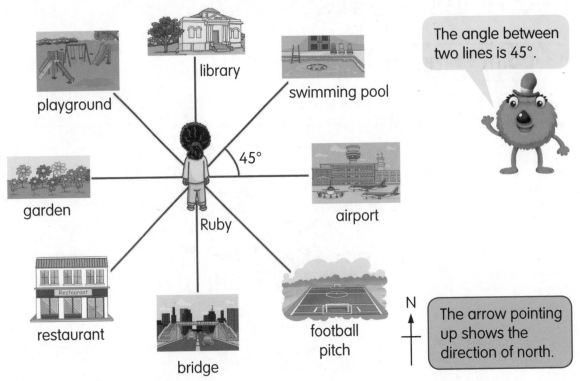

The angle between two lines is 45°.

The arrow pointing up shows the direction of north.

a Look at the places around Ruby. In which direction is each place from where she is standing?

   i The library is north of Ruby.

   ii The football pitch is south-east of Ruby.

   iii The playground is north-west of Ruby.

   iv The airport is east of Ruby.

b Use the picture above to complete the statements with the following words.

south-west	north-east	south-east
bridge	garden	airport

   i The restaurant is ☐ of Ruby.   **ii** The ☐ is south of Ruby.

   iii The swimming pool is ☐ of Ruby.   **iv** The ☐ is west of Ruby.

4 Look at the picture on page 128 again.

a If Ruby turns 90° clockwise, she will face the airport.

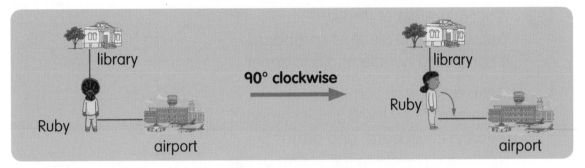

b Ruby is facing north. If she turns 90° anti-clockwise, she will face the garden.

c Ruby is facing north. If she turns 45° clockwise, she will face the swimming pool.

d Ruby is facing south. If she turns 270° anti-clockwise, she will face the garden.

e Ruby is facing south-east. If she turns 135° anti-clockwise, she will face the [   ].

f Ruby is facing north-west. If she turns 180°, she will face the [   ].

g Ruby is facing [   ]. If she turns 135° clockwise, she will face the football pitch.

h Ruby is facing south. If she turns [   ]° clockwise, she will face the restaurant.

Activity

⑤   Work in groups of three.
You will need a piece of cardboard,
a cardboard needle and a fastener.

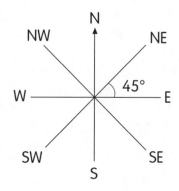

I   Make an 8-point compass
as shown. Copy the 8-point compass
onto the cardboard, and attach the
cardboard needle to the centre of the
compass with the fastener.

2   Take turns to use the compass. Copy and complete the table below.

Pupil	Start Position Facing	Turns Through an Angle of	End Position Facing
A	north	45° clockwise	
B	south-west	315° anti-clockwise	
C	east	135° clockwise	
A		225° anti-clockwise	north-east
B		90° clockwise	south
C		360°	north-west
A	west		south-east
B	north-west		south-west
C	east		west

Home Maths

Give your child a compass and ask them to face north.
Help them to describe their surroundings using the
words: north, south, east, west, north-east, north-west,
south-east, south-west, clockwise and anti-clockwise.

6 You can also tell the direction of one object from another object.

a Look at the dots below.

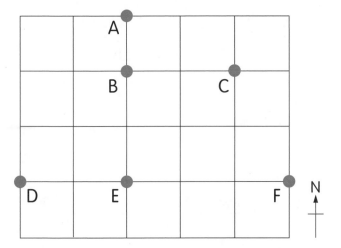

i Dot E is south of Dot B.

ii Dot B is north of Dot E.

iii Dot B is north-east of Dot D.

iv Dot A is north of Dot E.

v Dot E is south-west of Dot C.

vi Dot F is south-east of Dot A.

b Use the following words or letters to complete the statements below.

east	north-west	north-east	south-east
D	E	B	F

i Dot C is [ ] of Dot B.

ii Dot [ ] is west of Dot E.

iii Dot C is north-east of Dot [ ].

iv Dot A is [ ] of Dot F.

Practice Book 4A, p.119

Put On Your Thinking Caps!

7 **a** You are standing at point X and facing south.
You make a $\frac{3}{4}$ turn in a clockwise direction.

Then you make a $\frac{1}{2}$ turn clockwise.

Which direction will you be facing?

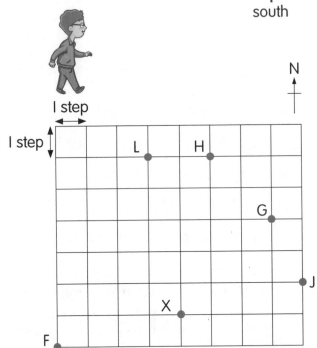

b Look at the diagram on the right and answer the following questions.

I step

I step

Peter was at a certain position. He walked in the following directions and ended up at position X:

2 steps to the north, then 2 steps to the west,
then 2 steps to the south, then I step to the east,
then I step to the south, and then 3 steps to the west.

Which letter marks his starting position?

Practice Book 4A, p.123

Practice Book 4A, p.124

Perpendicular and Parallel Lines

Let's Learn!

Drawing perpendicular lines

1 To draw perpendicular lines, you need a set-square and a ruler.

1 Draw a straight line AB using a ruler.

or

A ——————————— B

2 Place a set-square against the line AB.

or

3 Use the edge of the set-square to draw a line.

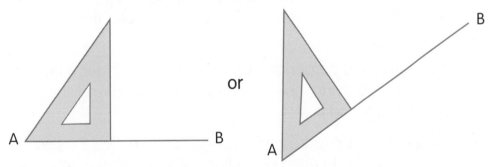

or

The lines AB and CD are perpendicular lines.

133

2 Draw a line perpendicular to the line AB through the point X.

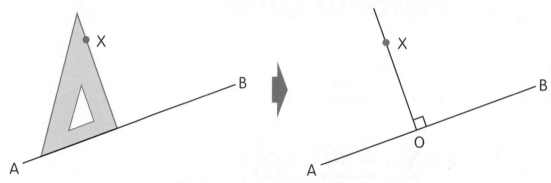

Slide the set-square along the line AB until the edge of the set-square touches the point X. Then draw a line at O through X to meet the line AB.

The line OX is perpendicular to the line AB.

Activity

3 **a** Draw a straight line. Ask your partner to draw a line perpendicular to your line. Take turns to draw perpendicular lines.

b Draw a straight line and mark a point near it. Ask your partner to draw a line perpendicular to the first line through the point. Take turns to mark points and draw lines perpendicular to the first line through the points.

c You will need square grid paper as shown. Draw a line perpendicular to each given line without using a set-square. Explain how you drew the lines.

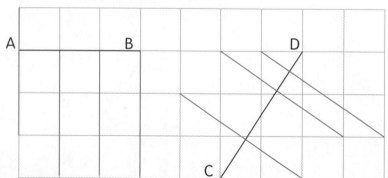

4 Copy each of these lines and mark point A. Use a set-square to draw a line perpendicular to the given line.
Start at the point A of each given line.

a

b

5 Copy each of these lines and mark point X. Use a set-square to draw a line perpendicular to the given line through the point X.

a

b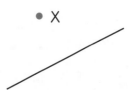

Practice Book 4A, p.133

Let's Learn!

Drawing parallel lines

1 To draw a parallel line you need a set-square and a ruler.

1 Draw a straight line with a ruler.

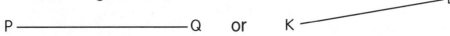

P ——————————— Q   or   K ———————— L

2 Place a set-square against the line. Then place a ruler against the side of the set-square as shown.

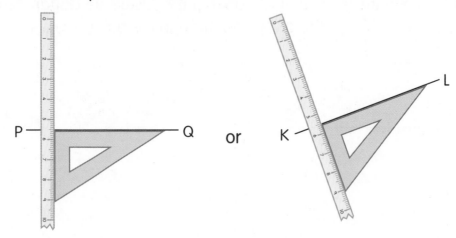

or

3 Slide the set-square along the ruler. Then use the edge of the set-square to draw a line MN or IJ.

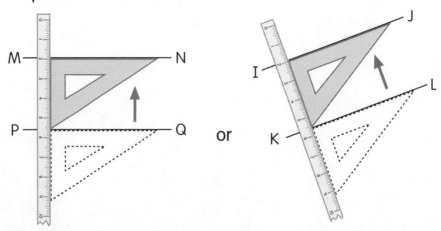

or

The lines PQ and MN are parallel lines.
The lines KL and IJ are parallel lines.

2 This is how to draw a line parallel to CD through the point R.

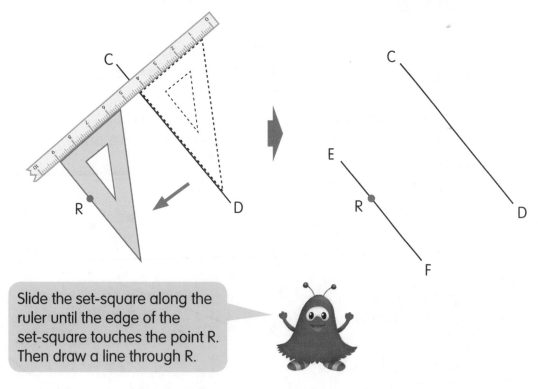

> Slide the set-square along the ruler until the edge of the set-square touches the point R. Then draw a line through R.

The line EF is parallel to the line CD.

3 PQR is a triangle.

Copy the triangle PQR on a piece of paper.

a Use a set-square and a ruler to draw:

    i a line parallel to the line QR through the point P.

    ii a line parallel to the line PQ through the point R.

b What do you notice about the two lines you have drawn?

c What do you notice about the shape you have drawn?

Activity

4 **a** Work in pairs. Draw a straight line, and ask your partner to draw a line parallel to your line. Take turns to draw parallel lines.

b Draw a straight line and mark a point near it. Ask your partner to draw a line parallel to the first line through the point. Take turns to mark points and draw lines parallel to the first line through the points.

c On a sheet of paper, copy the line EF and the dots as shown. Draw lines parallel to EF. Each parallel line you draw should pass through one of the points given.

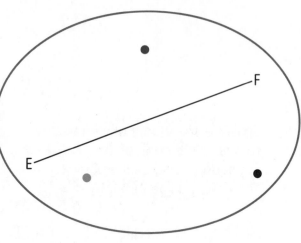

Practice Book 4A, p.135

Let's Learn!

Horizontal and vertical lines

1 The rectangle ABCD is drawn on a piece of paper pinned on a wall.

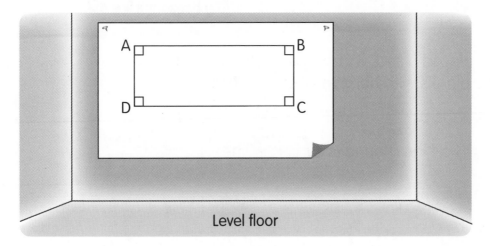

Level floor

The lines AB and DC are parallel to the floor.
Both AB and DC are said to be **horizontal** lines.
Lines AD and BC meet the horizontal lines AB and DC at right angles.
Both AD and BC are said to be **vertical** lines.

2 Look at the picture below. Find the vertical and horizontal lines in it.
What can you say about these lines?

A line on or parallel to the level ground is a horizontal line. A line perpendicular to the level ground is a vertical line.

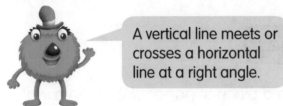

A vertical line meets or crosses a horizontal line at a right angle.

A vertical line is always perpendicular to a horizontal line.

3 Hannah placed a stick XY upright on the ground. Fill in the blanks with **horizontal** and **vertical**.

The stick XY is a [ ] line.

The line AB on the ground is a [ ] line.

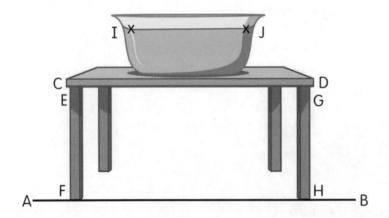

4 In the picture below, there is a basin of water on the table. List all the horizontal lines and vertical lines in the picture.

Home Maths

Encourage your child to look around them and identify horizontal and vertical lines.

Practice Book 4A, p.137

Put On Your Thinking Caps!

5 X is a point near the line AB.

 X

A ——————————————— B

Copy the line AB and the point X on a piece of paper.

a Draw a line perpendicular to the line AB through the point X.

b Then use a set-square and a ruler to draw two more lines to make a rectangle.

Practice Book 4A, p.139   Practice Book 4A, p.140

Squares and Rectangles

Let's Learn!

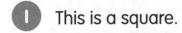
Squares and rectangles

1 This is a square.

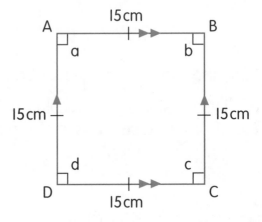

A square is a 4-sided shape.

It has 4 equal sides.
AB = BC = CD = DA

We draw the black lines to show that the lengths of all sides are equal.

Its opposite sides are parallel lines.
This means it has 2 pairs of parallel sides.
AB // DC and AD // BC

We draw the arrowheads to show that the opposite sides are parallel lines.

It has 4 right angles.
$\angle a = \angle b = \angle c = \angle d = 90°$

2 This is a rectangle.

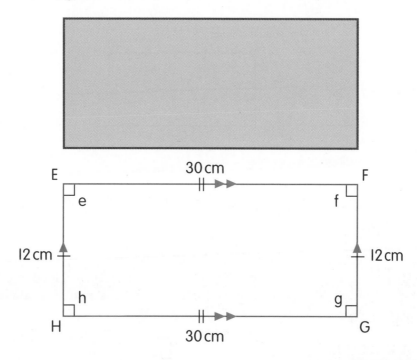

A rectangle is a 4-sided shape.

Its opposite sides are equal.
EF = HG
EH = FG

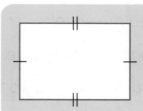

We draw the black lines to show that the lengths of opposite sides are equal.

Its opposite sides are parallel lines.
This means it has 2 pairs of parallel sides.
EF // HG and EH // FG

It has 4 right angles.
∠e = ∠f = ∠g = ∠h = 90°

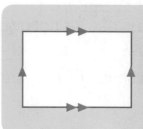

We draw the arrowheads to show that the opposite sides are parallel lines.

Home Maths

Encourage your child to name five things which have the shape of a square and five things which have the shape of a rectangle in your home.

3 These are some shapes drawn on a square grid.

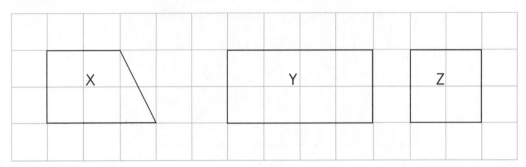

Look at the shapes. Copy and complete the table to show the properties of each shape.

Property	Shape		
	X	Y	Z
It has four sides	✓	✓	✓
All sides are equal	☐	☐	☐
Opposite sides are equal	☐	☐	☐
Exactly one pair of parallel sides	☐	☐	☐
Exactly two pairs of parallel sides	☐	☐	☐
All angles are right angles	☐	☐	☐

Shape ☐ is a square.

Shape ☐ is a rectangle.

Shape ☐ is not a square or a rectangle.

4 Which shape is a square? How do you identify a square?

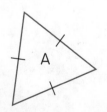
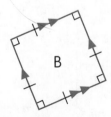
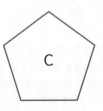
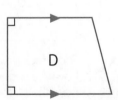

5 Which shape is a rectangle? How do you identify a rectangle?

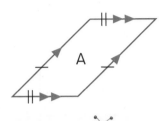 A

 B

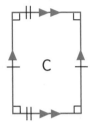 C

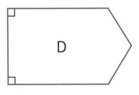 D

Activity

6 Use a geoboard and a rubber band to make these shapes. Which shapes are squares? Which shapes are rectangles?

You may copy the shapes onto square dotty paper. Then use a set-square and ruler to help you identify the shapes.

a
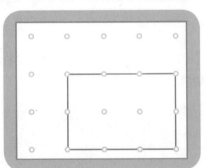

b
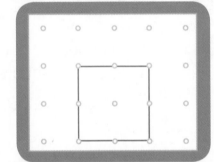

c
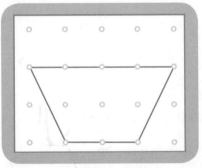

d
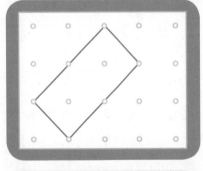

e
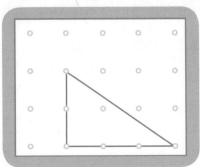

f
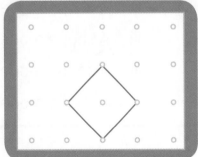

7 Find the lengths of the unknown sides.

a Shape JKLM is a square.

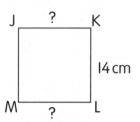

b Shape PQRS is a rectangle.

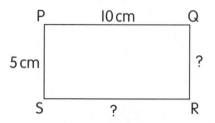

JK = [ ] cm

LM = [ ] cm

QR = [ ] cm

RS = [ ] cm

Activity

8 **a** Use a geoboard and two rubber bands to make this shape made up of a square and a rectangle.

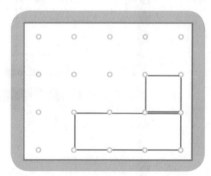

You may copy the shapes onto square dotty paper.

b Make the following shapes on the geoboard:

i A shape made from 2 rectangles.

ii A shape made from 1 rectangle and 2 squares.

iii A shape made from 1 square and 2 rectangles.

iv A shape made from 4 squares.

v A shape made from 4 rectangles.

9 Find the unknown sides of the rectangles and squares.

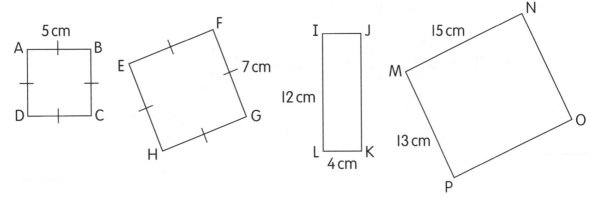

Let's Explore!

10 **a** Work in pairs. You will need straws of the following lengths:

4 cm, 4 cm, 4 cm, 4 cm, 6 cm, 6 cm, 6 cm, 6 cm, 8 cm, 8 cm

1 Make two squares and two rectangles with these straws. You can only use one or two straws to make each side of the shape.

2 Draw the shapes and label their sides on a piece of paper.

3 Compare your shapes with the shapes made by the other groups.

b Draw these shapes. Each of the shapes is made of a square and a rectangle.

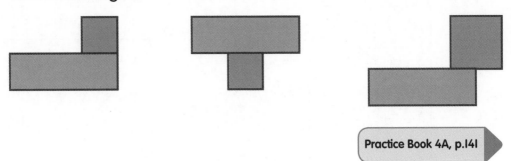

Practice Book 4A, p.141

147

Let's Learn!

More on squares and rectangles

1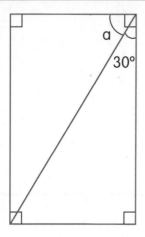

A square or a rectangle has 4 right angles.

Find ∠a.

∠a = 90° − 30°
= 60°

2 Find the unknown angles marked in the squares and rectangles below. The following shapes are not drawn to scale.

a

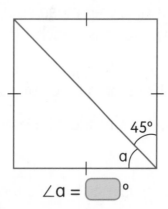

∠a = ⬡ °

b

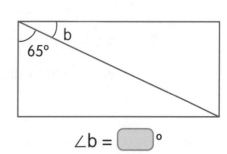

∠b = ⬡ °

c

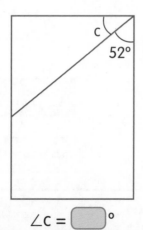

∠c = ⬡ °

d

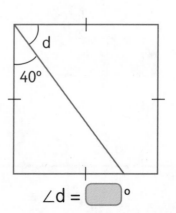

∠d = ⬡ °

3 Shape ABCDEF is made up of two rectangles. Find the length of BC.

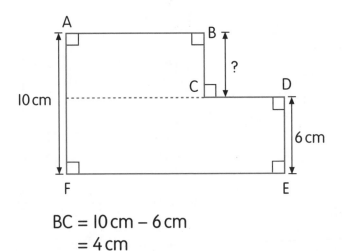

The opposite sides of a rectangle are equal.

BC = 10 cm − 6 cm
    = 4 cm

4 Shape GHIJKL is made up of a square and a rectangle.
Find the length of IJ.

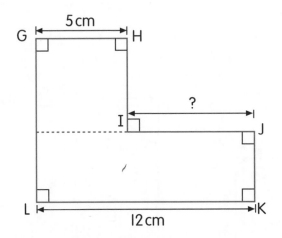

The sides of a square are all equal.

IJ = 12 cm − 5 cm
   = 7 cm

5 Find the unknown lengths in each of the following shapes.

a

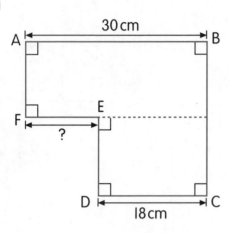

FE = ☐ cm

b

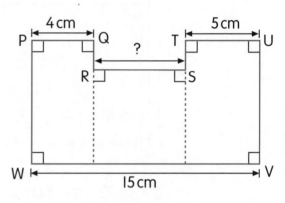

RS = ☐ cm

6 All lines in the shapes below meet at right angles. Find the unknown length for each shape.

a

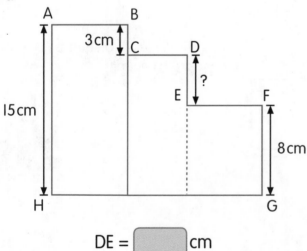

DE = ☐ cm

b

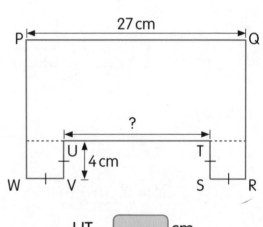

UT = ☐ cm

Activity

7 Work in pairs. You will need a sheet of I cm square grid paper.
On the grid paper, draw two different shapes made up of squares
and rectangles.

a What is the length around each shape?

b Write the lengths of all the sides.

Example

The total perimeter of each shape is 16 cm.

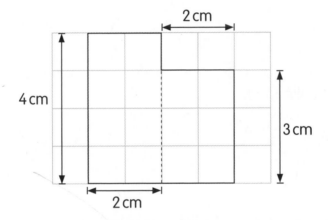

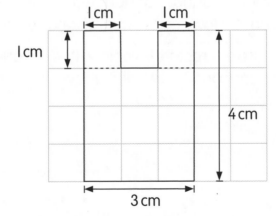

Practice Book 4A, p.145

Put On Your Thinking Caps!

8 **a** Which 8 sticks must you remove to leave behind 2 squares?

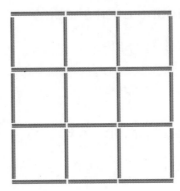

b Emma has some squares of side 1 cm and rectangles of side 3 cm by 1 cm like these:

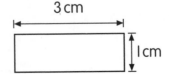

Help Emma make a square of side 3 cm using the squares and rectangles above. How many squares and rectangles did you use?

Help Emma make a rectangle of length 4 cm and width 3 cm using the squares and rectangles above. How many squares and rectangles did you use?

Practice Book 4A, p.150   Practice Book 4A, p.151